UNFINISHED CHAPTERS: COMPLETING CLAYTON'S LEGACY

Unfinished Chapters: Completing Clayton's Legacy

A WIFE'S JOURNEY THROUGH LOVE, LOSS, AND EMPOWERMENT

Lucy S. Desmore

Author

Bethune Publishing House, Inc.

Contents

Forward	1
Me And My Love	6
1 The Foundation of Legacy	7
New Beginnings	20
2 The Pillars of Strength	22
3 The Wealth of Knowledge	35
4 Challenges and Triumphs: The Stepping Stones	47
5 The Harmony of Love and Loss	57
6 Seeds of Hope: Planting the Future Together	66
We Remember - Veterans Memorial	77
7 Exploring Ancestral Wisdom: Journey to the Roots	79
Community Recognition	89
8 The Currency of Knowledge	91
Still We Press Forward	102
9 The Art of Perseverance	105
10 The Harmony of Health and Wealth	117
11 The Echoes of Empowerment - Voices of the Vanguard: Leading with Purpose"	127
Clay - Back In The Day	134

I Thought About You Today - Jozie B 135
Who Is Lucy Stewart Desmore 137

Forward

In the pages of "Unfinished Chapters: Completing Clayton's Legacy – A Wife's Journey Through Love, Loss, and Empowerment," Lucy S. Desmore weaves a tapestry of resilience, unity, and transformative power that resonates deeply with the principles my great-grandmother, Dr. Mary McLeod Bethune, championed throughout her life. It is with a profound sense of honor and responsibility that I pen this forward, recognizing the parallel paths of our ancestors' dreams and the embodiment of those dreams within this remarkable narrative.

Lucy S. Desmore's journey, meticulously chronicled within these pages, is more than a memoir; it is a beacon of hope and a testament to the indomitable spirit of love and community empowerment. As I looked closely at Lucy's and Clayton's stories, I was moved by the depth of their partnership, their shared vision, and the legacy they aspired to build – not just for themselves but for their community at large. Their story is a vivid illustration of the African proverb, "If you want to go fast, go alone; if you want to go far, go together."

Clayton Desmore's vision, as brought to life by Lucy, was steeped in the belief that a legacy of empowerment is forged through the collective efforts of love, faith, and unwavering commitment to community. This belief mirrors the ethos of my great-grandmother, Dr. Mary McLeod Bethune, who devoted her life to the education and advancement of African Americans, particularly women. Both Clayton and Dr. Bethune understood that true empowerment comes from lifting others, from planting seeds of hope and nurturing them into pillars of strength and beacons of progress.

Through the trials and triumphs shared in "Unfinished Chapters," Lucy invites us into the heart of their journey, showcasing the resilience required to navigate the storms of life. The narrative is a powerful reminder that adversity, while inevitable, offers a canvas upon which the most profound tales of human strength are painted. Clayton and Lucy's response to personal loss, community challenges, and the trials of entrepreneurship is a testament to their unbreakable bond and their unwavering commitment to their shared vision.

What strikes me most profoundly about Lucy's narrative is the undercurrent of forgiveness and renewal that courses through their story. Clayton's journey toward forgiving himself, laying his son's headstone, and moving forward echoes the essence of healing and personal growth. This process of forgiveness is a cornerstone of empowerment, allowing us to release the weights that tether us to the past and embark on a path of purpose and possibility.

The legacy of Clayton and Lucy Desmore, as encapsulated in this book, is a clarion call to all of us to reflect on the roots from which we have grown, to embrace the power of community, and to contribute to a legacy that transcends individual achievement. Their story is a reminder that the fabric of a community is strengthened not by its most illustrious threads but by the collective weave of its diverse and resilient members.

As the CEO of The Dr. Mary McLeod Bethune Family Legacy, Inc., I am continually inspired by stories of individuals who embody the principles of empowerment, education, and community upliftment that Dr. Bethune held dear. "Unfinished Chapters" is a shining example of how personal narratives can inspire collective action and enduring change. Lucy S. Desmore has not only shared her and Clayton's story with us; she has extended an invitation to join in the ongoing journey of building communities where dreams can flourish, and legacies can be built.

It is my hope that readers of "Unfinished Chapters" will be moved not only by the depth of Lucy's love and resilience but also by the call to action that her story represents. May we all be inspired to plant our seeds of hope, nurture our communities with love and faith, and contribute to a legacy of empowerment that will resonate for generations to come.

In closing, I am reminded of Dr. Mary McLeod Bethune's enduring words: "We have a powerful potential in our youth, and we must have the courage to change old ideas and practices so that we may direct their power toward good ends." "Unfinished Chapters: Completing Clayton's Legacy" embodies this powerful potential, illustrating the courage to change, the strength found in unity, and the endless possibilities that emerge when we dedicate ourselves to the upliftment of others.

In the spirit of Dr. Mary McLeod Bethune, let us move forward, guided by the legacy of Clayton and Lucy Desmore, and continue the work of building a future where every individual has the opportunity to thrive, empowered by the love and support of their community.

Keep Looking Up,
Dr. Evelyn Bethune
www.bethuneblueprint.org
drevelyn@greatnessdna.com

Deep Roots - Strong Tree
Bethune Publishing

A Wife's Journey Through Love, Loss, and Empowerment
By Lucy Stewart Desmore *With Love*

Not Good Bye- Just See Your Later
Bothuno Publishing

Me and My Love

1

The Foundation of Legacy

AFFIRMATION:

"Through every challenge and triumph, our shared vision and resilience illuminate the path to a legacy of empowerment, unity, and endless possibilities. Together, we sow the seeds of hope, nurturing a future where dreams take root in the strength of community."

Clayton's Vision

In the twilight of his life, Clayton Desmore left us with a narrative that was as much a beacon for the future as it was a reflection on the past. His book, "Dad, The Man, The Myth, The Legend," concluded with a poignant moment of closure and introspection at the resting place of his son, Nicky. It was a testament to Clayton's enduring spirit, a promise made under the weight of immense grief and love. This promise was not just about a physical monument but symbolized the laying of a foundation for a legacy that would outlive him. The journey of fulfilling this promise was marked by both personal and communal triumphs, a story that I, as his wife, have the privilege and responsibility to continue.

Clayton's vision was rooted in the belief that legacy is built on the pillars of love, faith, and community. He envisioned a future where the struggles and victories of Black families were not just individual tales of perseverance but collective stories of empowerment. This vision was deeply influenced by the narrative-driven and empowering style of authors like Iyanla Vanzant, whose work "One Day My Soul Opened Up" resonated with Clayton's desire for personal and communal healing. Similarly, the movie "The Pursuit of Happyness" mirrored Clayton's own life story, illustrating the profound impact of determination and resilience in the face of adversity.

Our venture into the world of entrepreneurship with "CLD Hair and Beauty Supplies" was a bold step towards realizing Clayton's dream. Located near the heartbeat of our community, Bethune-Cookman University, our store was more than just a business; it was a platform for engaging with and serving our community. Despite the challenges, from the economic constraints to the devastating effects of natural disasters like Hurricane Katrina, we remained steadfast. The decision to contribute to the relief efforts in New Orleans was a reflection of Clayton's ethos – that in times of need, communities must come together to support one another.

The transition from the small but mighty premises of our first store to the larger space of the new "CLD Hair and Beauty Store" marked a significant milestone in our journey. This move was not just about expanding our business but about creating a space that embodied the essence of community and legacy. The inclusion of a barber and beautician, alongside a selection of clothing, was a step towards creating a holistic community hub, a place where individuals could not only find products that met their physical needs but also experience a sense of belonging and cultural connection.

However, the journey was not without its trials. The hurricane season, particularly the impact of Katrina, tested our resilience. The physical damage to our store and the subsequent closure was a stark reminder of the transient nature of material possessions. Yet, it also highlighted the indomitable spirit of our community and the strength that lies in unity and collective action.

As we navigated the aftermath of the storm and the eventual closure of our store, I found myself at a crossroads. The question of "What now?" loomed large. It was a moment that called for introspection and a return to the foundational values that Clayton and I had always held dear. My foray into the realm of real estate and the decision to focus on health were steps towards adapting to the new realities of our lives while staying true to our vision.

Reflecting on Clayton's legacy and the journey we embarked on together, I am reminded of the power of dreams and the importance of keeping promises. The laying of Nicky's headstone was not just an act of closure but a reaffirmation of our commitment to building a legacy that transcends time and circumstance. In Clayton's words,

"The last chapter of the first book ended speaking of a laying of the headstone at Nicky's resting place. It took about fifteen years to get the strength to do it. For the first seven years, I was lost because I had not accepted his being gone. My spirit could not release his spirit to do anything. I could not celebrate anything without guilt such as our Anniversary and Father's Day. There will be times when you cannot do things you want because mental or physical powers are the worst and you must wait them out.

I invite you to reflect on your own roots. We all have things that sometimes keep us stuck. FORGIVENESS will free you and help you to move forward as it did Clay. Clay was open to receiving the message that God gave him and to not just hear but to move on it. Let Clayton's story and our continued journey inspire you to pursue your aspirations with courage, determination, and an unwavering faith in the power of love and community.

Let's look deeper into the essence of community building, the challenges and rewards of entrepreneurship, and the significance of passing the baton to the next generation. Every remarkable story begins with a dream, a vision that becomes its driving force. Clayton, my beloved husband, was the embodiment of such a dreamer. His vision, deeply embedded in the heart of our community and our family, was a guiding light that led us through both joyous and challenging times. This vision wasn't just his alone; it evolved into a shared dream, especially between us.

Clayton's journey reminded me of those grand epics where heroes rise from humble origins, destined for greatness. His dreams were never self-centered; they were always about lifting others along with him. As a young man, he witnessed the disparities in our community. Yet, he chose to see these not as insurmountable obstacles but as opportunities for growth and empowerment.

One of the most poignant aspects of Clayton's life was his relationship with his son, Nicky. Nicky, with his infectious smile and indomitable spirit, despite his disabilities, was a living testament to Clayton's belief in strength and unconditional love. Witnessing their bond taught me so much about resilience and finding joy in every moment, no matter how challenging.

My entry into Clayton's life added a new dimension to his vision. I wasn't just a partner in love but also in purpose. Together, we formed a synergy, his roots providing stability and my wings offering us the chance to soar to new heights. Our dreams are intertwined, founded on shared values and aspirations.

Our shared dream went beyond our personal lives and extended into the heart of our community. Establishing CLD Hair and Beauty Supplies was more than opening a business; it was about creating a community space that mirrored our culture, values, and dreams. It was our way of giving back, of crafting a legacy that resonated with our people.

The unexpected loss of Nicky was a profound turning point. It served as a painful reminder of life's fragility and the urgency of creating a lasting legacy. Nicky's spirit – resilient, loving, and determined – became a part of everything we did, adding depth and meaning to our endeavors.

Clayton often found wisdom in Ann Patchett's words about forgiveness and self-compassion. These principles guided us, particularly during moments of doubt and introspection. They reminded us that our life's tapestry was still being woven, with each choice and experience adding to its richness.

Clayton's vision, now deeply intertwined with my own, kept evolving. It transcended the bounds of mere business success or personal comfort; it was about forging a legacy that would endure. Our dream was about empowerment – not just for ourselves but for everyone who joined us on this journey.

Standing beside Clayton, watching the sunset over the community we cherished and served, I knew our story was far from over. Many more chapters awaited, dreams to be realized, and legacies to be built. Clayton's vision remained our guiding light, a beacon not just for us but for future generations to follow.

The Power of Community

Community is the soil in which our dreams grow. Clayton and I always believed in the power of the people around us – our neighbors, friends, and even those we just passed on the street. It was in the everyday interactions, the shared struggles, and the collective triumphs that our vision for a better future was nurtured.

I remember vividly the day Clayton and I got married. The community's outpouring of love was overwhelming. Our wedding wasn't just a union of two souls; it was a celebration of collective joy. However, our journey together wasn't only about joyful celebrations. We faced our share of sorrows, too, most notably the heart-wrenching loss of Nicky. It was during these moments of profound grief that the true strength of our community shone through. Their support was a balm, a reminder that we were not alone in our journey.

Grieving is a process that takes one through various stages of pain, reflection, and, eventually, healing. Clayton and I experienced this firsthand after Nicky's passing. As we navigated our grief, the community's role was indispensable. They provided a listening ear, a shoulder to cry on, and, most importantly, a shared understanding of our loss. This collective healing process was a testament to the strength and resilience inherent in our community.

Opening CLD Hair and Beauty Supplies was a dream come true. It was more than just a business; it was a place where community members could come together, share stories, and support each other. I recall how our store became a hub of activity, a place buzzing with life, laughter, and the shared experiences of our people. It was here that we truly saw the impact of our work, not just as entrepreneurs but as community builders.

UNFINISHED CHAPTERS: COMPLETING CLAYTON'S LEGACY

Our involvement in the community was not limited to the business. Clayton and I actively engaged in community events, fundraisers, and initiatives that aimed to uplift and empower our people. We believed that empowerment wasn't just about financial success; it was about giving people the tools to shape their own destinies. This belief was at the core of everything we did, from the products we sold in our store to the conversations we had with every person who walked through our doors.

Looking back, I realize the profound impact our community had on us. In a way, they were co-authors of our story, contributing chapters filled with love, support, and shared wisdom. It was in these interactions that Clayton's and my vision for a better future found its true meaning. As Ann Patchett once said, "The ability to forgive oneself...is the key to making art, and very possibly the key to finding any semblance of happiness in life." This quote resonates with me as I reflect on our journey, understanding that our community helped us forgive, heal, and grow.

Our journey was not without challenges. We faced obstacles, both personal and communal. But it was in overcoming these challenges that our bond with the community was strengthened. Every triumph, no matter how small, was a victory for all of us. We celebrated together, knowing that each success was a step toward a greater goal.

As I look to the future, I am filled with hope and determination. The legacy that Clayton and I have built is not just about us; it's about the community that supported us, grew with us, and believed in our vision. The power of community is a force that can move mountains, break barriers, and create lasting change. It is this power that will continue to drive our dreams and aspirations forward.

In the end, the power of community is the most potent force for change. It is in our collective strength, shared dreams, and united efforts that we find the true essence of empowerment. Clayton's and my story is a testament to this power – a story that will continue to inspire and guide future generations in our community and beyond.

Building from the Ground Up

Starting a small business as a Black owner in Daytona Beach was nothing like we dreamed. My husband Clayton and I faced this when we opened CLD Hair and Beauty Supplies. It was tough, with challenges not just in running the business but also in getting support from the community we wanted to serve.

We had a big dream. Our store wasn't meant to be just a place to shop; we wanted it to be a cornerstone of our community, reflecting our culture and values. But reality hit us hard. Despite people saying nice things, their support often didn't translate into them shopping with us. This gap between what people said and what they did was a hard lesson in the realities of community and business.

We hoped our community would rally around us, making our success a shared victory. But the support we expected often fell short in Daytona Beach. It was tough realizing that our communal dream might not be as shared as we thought.

I remember quitting my teaching job in Sanford to start the store with Clayton. He thought of the idea when I came home frustrated from a hair store one day. It seemed like a wild idea at first, but we jumped in – quitting my job and opening our store almost immediately. This was a big change, driven by our desire to control our destiny.

Running the store was unforgettable. Moving to a bigger space made us hopeful, but hearing someone thought we were closing was a stark reminder of our reality. "No one will be happy about your success except you," became a sobering truth we learned.

Amidst trying to grow our business, we faced personal tragedies that shook us. The death of my father-in-law was particularly tough, coming on top of other losses. These times tested our faith, drawing Clayton and me closer as we supported each other through the grief. Through all this, running the store taught us deep lessons about resilience, the true nature of dreams, and the importance of perseverance. Success felt more like a personal journey, often lonely and misunderstood, but it was ours to make.

Clayton often reflected on the journey, drawing inspiration from the idea that forgiving ourselves and finding happiness along the way was crucial. This mindset helped us view our challenges as parts of a larger story we were living. Building CLD Hair and Beauty Supplies from scratch was more than just an entrepreneurial venture; it was a deep dive into the realities of life, business, and community engagement. Despite the hurdles, our story is one of persistence, a reminder that true success is often accompanied by unexpected challenges.

Passing the Baton

Think of the best advice or lesson you've ever received. Sharing wisdom and strength with others is one of the most powerful gifts we can give. Clayton and my life story is full of ups and downs, and through it all, we've gathered lots of wisdom we want to pass on. We see our lives like a storybook, filled with lessons we hope the next generation can use to write their own stories.

Our tale isn't just about the business we ran or the personal losses we faced; it's about how tough we were when things got hard. Every tough time we went through taught us something about not giving up, and showing what people can do when they really try.

Through every problem, being resilient and keeping faith were our secret weapons. They were like the glue holding our story together. When things felt too tough to handle, believing in ourselves and pushing forward helped us not just to get through but to come out stronger on the other side.

One thing became really clear to us: we had to share what we learned with kids and teens coming up after us. We didn't want to just leave behind things; we wanted to share the important lessons from our lives. This means talking about the hard times, the victories, and the priceless lessons we picked up along the way.

We didn't want our legacy to be just about us. We wanted to leave behind something lasting, something that future generations could use as a foundation to build their own dreams. Our legacy is more than just success; it's about working hard, helping out in the community, staying strong, and believing.

When I think back on our journey, I'm often reminded about how important it is to be kind to ourselves, a lesson I learned from Ann Patchett. Every step we took, every decision we made, was part of a bigger story. This helped us see the value in our experiences and the legacy we were creating.

Looking ahead, 'passing the baton' means giving the next bunch of kids and teens the wisdom and strength we've found. We want to empower them to tell their own stories, using the lessons from the past and the courage to try new things.

Life's like a relay race, and our turn to run is just one part of a much bigger story. As Clayton and I pass on our baton, we hope it helps the next generation go even further and higher than we did. The legacy we're leaving behind is filled with stories of toughness, faith, and never giving up, and now it's their turn to add to that legacy.

UNFINISHED CHAPTERS: COMPLETING CLAYTON'S LEGACY

The Essence of Our Story

It's crucial to look back and see what we've gone through together. Clayton's and my journey has been about love, overcoming losses, empowering ourselves and our community, and staying strong through it all. From starting our business, and facing community challenges, to sharing our lessons with others, our story is a testament to what people can achieve when they stick together and keep pushing forward.

Our story isn't just ours; it's been shaped by everyone around us, even when things didn't go as planned. The journey of starting and running our business, alongside our personal battles, taught us invaluable lessons about life, the importance of sticking to your path, and helping others along the way.

One of the biggest takeaways from our story is how important it is to leave something meaningful behind—a legacy. Our experiences, both good and bad, are lessons we're passing on. How we dealt with challenges and kept our faith shows the kind of legacy we want to leave: one of resilience, hard work, and hope.

We're determined to share our journey with the younger generation. It's about giving more than just stuff; it's about passing on the wisdom we've gained. We want to inspire you to face your own challenges, learn from them, and grow stronger.

Looking back, the journey we've shared has been a complexity of life experiences. Remembering to be kind to ourselves and to find happiness in our path has been crucial. Every challenge, and every choice, has been a part of our unique story, helping us appreciate the journey and the legacy we're building.

Now, it's your turn. Think about the legacy you want to create. What lessons from your life do you want to share? How can you use your experiences to strengthen yourself and help others? Life is a relay race, and now you're holding the baton.

The baton we're passing on is more than a symbol of our achievements; it's a beacon of hope and guidance for what's to come. As Clayton and I hand over our baton, we do so with the hope that it lights your way, encouraging you to run your race with courage, determination, and an unbreakable spirit.

New Beginnings

New Beginnings
Lucy Desmore

2

The Pillars of Strength

AFFIRMATION:

"In unity, we find strength. Together, we build not just a legacy but a fortress of support, understanding, and shared success. I am committed to fostering collaboration, embracing our collective wisdom, and contributing to a community where every member thrives. My actions are guided by love, my efforts are multiplied through partnership, and our achievements are a testament to our united spirit."

My Journey with Clayton

Life is a journey filled with stories, some told and many left unfinished. My journey with Clayton, my late husband, is a tale of love, struggle, and perseverance that I feel compelled to share. Our story, detailed in "Unfinished Chapters: Completing Clayton's Legacy," is not just our narrative but a beacon for others, especially for Black families and communities grappling with similar struggles and triumphs.

Clayton and I believed in the power of unity and community. We lived our lives trying to empower those around us, knowing well the obstacles we face as a community. This chapter, "United We Stand: Building Together," is close to my heart. It is about us — how we met, how we loved, and how we fought together for our dreams and those of our community. Booker T. Washington once said, "Success is to be measured not so much by the position that one has reached in life as by the obstacles which he has overcome." This quote resonates deeply with me. Clayton's and my story is a testament to overcoming obstacles, not just for personal success but for the upliftment of our community.

Our story begins at Bethune Cookman College, now University, in the Psychology Department, where we were both majoring in psychology. Clayton was already working at Daytona Beach Community College, and I returned to Bethune in 1980 to complete my studies. I graduated in the summer of 1982, and Clayton in the spring of 1985. Our academic advisor and one of our professors often hinted that Clayton had a soft spot for me, but I was too caught up in my world to notice. As an intern and a single mom, I was overwhelmed with responsibilities. Clayton, on the other hand, was navigating through his second marriage. Despite these complications, we found solace in our conversations about career paths and life. Clayton had this innate ability to listen and guide, making him not just an excellent academic advisor but also a great friend. Our friendship blossomed over the years, rooted in respect and mutual understanding.

In 1999, a whimsical decision to attend a service at Allen Chapel AME Church, following my mother's side of the family tradition, led me to cross paths with Clayton again. This encounter felt like destiny. He was there, welcoming guests and members at the entrance, and in that moment, something shifted within me. We began to see each other in a new light, not just as friends but as potential life partners. Our love story is not one of instant flames but a slow burn that grew stronger with time. Clayton proposed in February 2002, and we got married that June. Our marriage was a testament to our belief in love, unity, and the strength of partnership. We shared everything, from our love for music to our dreams of writing and leaving a legacy.

Clayton was not just my husband but my best friend, mentor, and partner in every sense. He taught me patience, resilience, and the importance of staying true to our goals. Together, we navigated the highs and lows of life, always emerging stronger. Our journey was not without its challenges, but it was our shared commitment to our community and to each other that kept us grounded. Clayton's work with the youth and our efforts to empower our community through education and mentorship were central to our lives. This chapter is not just a recount of our past but a message of hope and resilience. It's about the power of love and partnership in overcoming obstacles and building a legacy. As you read through our story, I hope you find inspiration in our journey and the courage to build your own legacy of love, unity, and community strength.

Synergy in the Community

When Clayton and I first started our journey together, one thing became crystal clear: the strength of a community lies in its unity. This belief was not just theoretical for us; it was a lived experience. "Synergy in the Community" is not just a section title; it's the essence of what Clayton and I strived to embody throughout our lives together. Our story of synergy began in the heart of Daytona Beach, where we both found our calling. I was a teacher, and Clayton was an academic advisor, but our roles extended far beyond these titles. We were connectors, builders of bridges between dreams and reality for the young minds we encountered. Our mission was to empower, to uplift, and to create spaces where every individual felt valued and heard.

The concept of synergy means that the whole is greater than the sum of its parts. For Clayton and me, this meant that our combined efforts could create something far more impactful than what we could achieve individually. We witnessed this first-hand when we started working on community projects. Whether it was mentoring youth, organizing educational workshops, or simply providing a listening ear, the impact of our joint efforts was palpable. Our approach to building community strength was rooted in the belief that education and understanding are the foundations upon which strong communities are built. We focused on creating opportunities for dialogue, for sharing stories, and for collective problem-solving. It was in these gatherings that we saw the true power of synergy come to life. People from different backgrounds, each with their unique struggles and triumphs, came together to support one another. This was unity in action.

Clayton had this remarkable ability to see potential in everyone. He believed that with the right guidance and support, anyone could overcome their obstacles and reach their full potential. This belief wasn't just empty words; it was reflected in his actions every day. He would spend hours counseling students, not just about their academic paths but about life's challenges. He was a mentor in the truest sense, guiding young individuals towards a brighter future. Our home became a hub for these community activities. It was a place where laughter and learning coexisted, where every person, regardless of their background, was welcomed with open arms. Clayton's charisma and my passion for education created a synergy that was infectious. We were not just a couple; we were a team dedicated to the upliftment of our community. One of the most significant projects we undertook was the establishment of a scholarship fund for local students. Education was a cause close to both our hearts, and we wanted to ensure that financial barriers did not hinder anyone's dream of pursuing higher education.

This scholarship fund was our way of giving back, of creating a legacy that would support the aspirations of young minds for generations to come. The synergy we created in our community was not just about the projects we initiated but about the relationships we built. It was about the trust we earned and the hope we instilled. Our journey together taught us that when individuals come together with a shared vision and purpose, there's no limit to what can be achieved. As I reflect on our journey, I am reminded of the countless lives we touched and the transformative power of collective action. Our story is a testament to the belief that unity, compassion, and dedication can create lasting change. It is a call to action for others to embrace the concept of synergy in their communities, to work together towards a common goal, and to build a legacy of empowerment and resilience. This section of our story is not just a look back at what we accomplished; it's an invitation to you, the reader, to find your own ways to contribute to the synergy in your community. Together, we can build stronger, more united communities that stand the test of time.

Overcoming Challenges Together

Clayton and I faced our fair share of challenges, both as individuals and as a couple. But it was our commitment to each other and to our community that helped us overcome each hurdle. This section, "Overcoming Challenges Together," is a testament to the resilience and unity we maintained through thick and thin. One of the earliest challenges we encountered was merging our lives together. Coming from different backgrounds and having both experienced failed marriages, we were cautious about blending our families and lives. However, we were determined to make it work. Our love for each other and for our community became the glue that held us together. We learned early on that communication and mutual respect were key to overcoming any obstacle.

As we navigated our journey, we encountered societal challenges that tested our resolve. Discrimination, economic hardships, and the struggle to maintain cultural identity in a rapidly changing world were constant battles. Yet, Clayton's wisdom and my passion for education guided us. We tackled each issue head-on, using them as opportunities to educate, to enlighten, and to empower those around us. Our approach to overcoming challenges was rooted in collective action. We believed that no challenge was too great when the community stood together. This belief was put to the test when we initiated a project to revitalize a local community center that had fallen into disrepair. The center had once been a hub for youth and families, offering programs and resources that supported the community's needs. Seeing its decline, we knew we had to act.

The project was daunting, and at times, it felt like we were fighting an uphill battle. Funding was scarce, and the bureaucratic red tape seemed endless. However, we refused to give up. We organized fundraising events, applied for grants, and rallied the community to volunteer their time and skills. It was a monumental effort that required patience, perseverance, and a lot of hard work. Through it all, Clayton's unshakeable faith and my determination kept us going. We faced each setback with resilience, learning from our failures and celebrating our victories, no matter how small. The community center project became a symbol of what could be achieved when we worked together, overcoming challenges through unity and shared purpose. Our personal challenges, too, were met with the same steadfast determination. Whether it was health scares, financial difficulties, or the loss of loved ones, we supported each other through every storm. Clayton's strength and my optimism were a powerful combination that helped us navigate the darkest of times.

One of the most significant challenges we faced was Clayton's illness. It was a battle we fought together, with the support of our community. Our family, friends, and even strangers rallied around us, offering their prayers, love, and support. It was during this time that we truly understood the depth of our impact on the community. The outpouring of love was overwhelming, and it gave us the strength to face each day with hope and courage. Through every challenge, Clayton and I learned valuable lessons about love, resilience, and the power of community. We realized that obstacles were not just hurdles to overcome but opportunities to grow stronger, both as individuals and as a couple. Our journey taught us that together, we could face anything life threw our way. As you, the reader, face your own challenges, remember that you are not alone. Lean on your community, embrace the support of loved ones, and never lose sight of your goals. Challenges are a part of life, but they do not define us. It is how we overcome them, together, that shapes our legacy.

The Role of Education

Education played a pivotal role in both Clayton's and my life. It was the beacon that guided us through our darkest days and the foundation upon which we built our dreams. This section, "The Role of Education," is not just about the academic learning we experienced but the lessons we learned outside the classroom that truly shaped our journey. Our belief in the power of education was rooted in our own experiences. Both of us understood that education was more than just acquiring knowledge; it was a tool for empowerment, a means to challenge the status quo, and a pathway to personal and community growth. We dedicated our lives to ensuring that those around us recognized and harnessed this power. Clayton's role as an academic advisor and my career as a teacher allowed us to directly impact the lives of countless young individuals. We saw firsthand the transformative effect of education on a person's life. It was not just about grades or degrees but about awakening a sense of curiosity, fostering critical thinking, and encouraging a lifelong love for learning.

Our approach to education was holistic. We believed in nurturing not just the mind but the soul. This meant addressing the socioeconomic barriers that many students in our community faced. We advocated for programs that provided not just academic support but also mental health resources, career counseling, and life skills training. It was important to us that education served as a ladder for upward mobility, offering a way out of poverty and a path to a brighter future. The synergy between education and community empowerment was evident in every project we undertook. From organizing literacy programs to setting up scholarship funds, our goal was always to uplift and empower. We understood that an educated community was a stronger community, one capable of advocating for its rights, challenging injustices, and paving the way for future generations.

Our work in the community taught us valuable lessons about the role of education in fostering unity and resilience. We learned that when people come together to learn, share, and grow, they create a powerful force for change. Education was our tool for building bridges, breaking down barriers, and creating a sense of belonging and purpose. One of the most rewarding aspects of our journey was witnessing the ripple effect of our efforts. We saw students who had benefited from our programs go on to achieve great things, returning to the community to give back and continue the cycle of empowerment. This was a testament to the enduring impact of education and its role in shaping leaders who are compassionate, informed, and committed to making a difference. As we navigated our own challenges, education remained our north star. It was a constant reminder of our purpose and the legacy we hoped to leave behind. Clayton's passion for writing and my love for teaching were not just personal pursuits but expressions of our belief in the transformative power of education.

To you, the reader, I extend an invitation to embrace education in all its forms. Seek knowledge, challenge yourself, and use your learning to make a positive impact in your community. Remember, education is not just a personal achievement but a tool for collective empowerment and change.

Legacy in Leadership

Clayton's and my journey was not just about the paths we walked; it was about the trails we blazed for others to follow. "Legacy in

Leadership" is a reflection on how our lives and actions shaped a legacy that, we hope, will inspire generations. This chapter is a testament to our belief that leadership is not about wielding power, but about empowering others. Our leadership style was deeply influenced by our experiences and the challenges we faced. We led by example, showing that resilience, compassion, and integrity were not just ideals but practical principles that guided our every action. Leadership, to us, was about lifting others as we climbed, ensuring that our journey was not a solitary climb to the top but a collective ascent where everyone's success was celebrated.

The legacy we aimed to leave was one of empowerment and community building. We understood that true leadership was about creating more leaders, not followers. This meant investing in people, recognizing their potential, and providing them with the tools and opportunities to succeed. Our work in education and community service was grounded in this philosophy. We sought to inspire a sense of responsibility and a commitment to positive change in everyone we worked with. Our leadership was also characterized by a commitment to authenticity and transparency. We shared our struggles and failures just as openly as our successes because we believed in the power of vulnerability. Showing that it's okay to stumble, to face challenges, and to be imperfect was a way to connect with others on a human level, fostering a culture of empathy and understanding.

In our community, we led initiatives that aimed not just to address immediate needs but to lay the groundwork for sustainable development. Whether it was through mentoring programs, educational scholarships, or community revitalization projects, our focus was always on the long-term impact. We wanted to leave a legacy that wasn't just about what we achieved but about what continued to grow from the seeds we planted. The leadership roles we assumed came with their share of challenges. We faced skepticism, resistance, and at times, outright opposition. Yet, it was our unwavering belief in our mission and the support of our community that kept us going. We learned that leadership was as much about listening as it was about leading. It was about being open to feedback, willing to adapt, and always prioritizing the greater good over personal accolades.

As we navigated the complexities of leadership, we were guided by the principle that the true measure of a leader is the legacy they leave behind. It's not about the titles held or the accolades received, but about the lives touched, the communities uplifted, and the positive changes that endure long after they're gone. Clayton and I lived our lives with this principle at the heart of everything we did. Our legacy, we hope, is one that will inspire others to lead with courage, compassion, and conviction. We hope it encourages others to see leadership not as a position of power but as an opportunity to serve, to contribute to something larger than themselves, and to make a lasting impact on the world.

To the reader, I leave you with this thought: leadership is not just for the selected few; it's a mantle that anyone can take up, in big ways and small, in your life and your community. The legacy you leave through your leadership is yours to shape. It's about the choices you make, the lives you touch, and the difference you make in the world. Let your legacy be one of empowerment, of making paths where there were none, and of leaving the world a little better than you found it.

Our Journey Forward

It's clear that the path Clay and I walked was paved with more than just our footsteps; it was built on our dreams, our struggles, and our victories. This story, our story, is not merely a recounting of past events but a blueprint for future generations. It's a narrative of hope, resilience, and the indomitable spirit of community. Our lives were intertwined in a mission that went beyond personal success. We sought to empower, to educate, and to lead in a manner that left a lasting impact on our community. From the classrooms where I taught to the counseling sessions Clayton led, every action was a step towards building a legacy. This legacy was not just about what we achieved but about the seeds of potential we planted in every life we touched.

The pillars of strength that supported our journey—synergy in the community, overcoming challenges together, the pivotal role of education, and a legacy in leadership—were not just chapters in our story. They were the very essence of our life's work. They represented our belief in the power of unity, the importance of perseverance, and the transformative impact of education and leadership. Our journey was a testament to the idea that true success is measured not by the wealth or accolades one accumulates but by the positive change one inspires in the world. It was a life lived in service to others, with the faith that even the smallest act of kindness can spark a wave of positive change.

As this chapter comes to a close, I find comfort in the knowledge that Clayton's and my journey does not end here. Our story, shared in these pages, continues in the lives of those we've touched, the community we've helped build, and the future leaders we've inspired. The legacy of Clayton Desmore, my beloved husband, partner, and best friend, lives on, not just in memory but in the ongoing work of empowerment and community building. The journey forward is one of continued commitment to the values we hold dear. It's a path of relentless pursuit of equality, empowerment, and excellence. It's a challenge to future generations to carry the torch we've passed on, to lead with compassion, and to create a world where every individual has the opportunity to thrive.

This story, our legacy, is now a part of a larger narrative—one of hope, transformation, and enduring love. It's a narrative that I invite others to join, to contribute their own chapters, and to continue the work that Clayton and I began. Together, united in purpose and action, we can build a future that honors the past and paves the way for a brighter tomorrow. As I move forward, with Clayton's spirit guiding me, I am reminded of the power of love, the importance of community, and the enduring impact of leaving a legacy that inspires others to dream more, learn more, do more, and become more. Our journey is a reminder that we are all authors of our own stories, capable of creating a legacy that transcends time.

Oh Happy Days

Clay and Lucy's Wedding Day
Lucy Desmore

3

The Wealth of Knowledge

AFFIRMATION:

"I am a beacon of knowledge and empowerment within my community, understanding that every book I read, every word I share, and every conversation I engage in plants seeds of wisdom and growth. I embrace the legacy of literacy, committed to expanding access to education and fostering a culture of learning that empowers individuals to shape their destinies and transform the world around them. Together, we are building a future where every voice is heard, every dream is valued, and every life is enriched through the power of education."

"Books and Bonds - A Library of Life"

I'm constantly reminded of the profound role education played in shaping not just Clayton's legacy, but our shared dreams and the lives we touched. From the very beginning, our paths were intertwined by a mutual understanding of a simple yet powerful truth, echoed by Nelson Mandela: "Education is the most powerful weapon which you can use to change the world." This belief became the cornerstone of our journey together, guiding us through the challenges and triumphs we faced as individuals and as a couple.

Our story is a testament to the transformative power of education. It's a narrative enriched by our reflections on "The Miseducation of the Negro" by Carter G. Woodson, which laid bare the systemic obstacles we, as a community, must navigate in our quest for enlightenment. The resilience of Dr. Mary McLeod Bethune, who fervently believed in literacy and education as tools for empowerment, always inspired us. Her determination resonated deeply with us, as she made it her mission to teach every Negro she could, highlighting the power of education to liberate.

Our educational journey began at Bethune-Cookman College, where fate had us meet. Our shared major in psychology was the first of many surprises. I pursued teaching, while Clayton was already making his mark as an advisor and counselor. It was ironic how our lives, though on different paths, converged in the psychology department. Clayton's gesture of leaving a sausage biscuit on my chair every day was more than just an act of kindness; it was a symbol of the thoughtful and caring person he was, always looking to nurture and support those around him.

The significance of attending a historically Black university was not lost on us, especially Clayton. He had initially considered attending what is now the University of Central Florida, but the legacy of attending a historically Black university, a tradition in his family, was too important to forego. Education, for us, was not just about acquiring knowledge; it was about understanding our history, our culture, and the power of our voices.

Books were more than just decoration in our home; they were windows to the world, tools for engagement and intellectual growth. Clayton didn't just collect books; he engaged with them, using them as a means to spark intelligent conversations and challenge perspectives. His belief that knowledge stored in the mind was something no one could take away was a guiding principle in our lives.

We didn't solely focus on our personal growth but on how we could contribute to the community's development. From starting the CDL Beauty Store to creating Tomorrow's Vision, Inc., we were driven by the dream of making a difference, one step at a time. Our ventures were not just businesses; they were platforms for empowerment, for creating opportunities, and for fostering a spirit of self-reliance and community support.

As I share our story, it's not just a recollection of what was but a beacon for what can be. Education, as we've lived and understood it, is a key to freedom, a means to unlock the potential within each of us and our community. It's a legacy that Clayton and I believed in deeply, one that we've strived to pass on to our children and to every life we've touched.

Reading Books Plants Seeds

I can't help but reflect on the seeds of knowledge these volumes represented in our lives. Books were more than mere objects to us; they were vessels of wisdom, gateways to worlds unknown, and they opened doors to greater possibilities. Clayton loved reading, a habit that I admired and shared. Among the many titles that lined our shelves, three books, in particular, stood out, not just for their content but for the profound impact they had on us, individually and as a couple.

"Rule Your Day" by Joel Osteen was a beacon of positivity in our home. Clayton would often quote Osteen in our morning conversations, reminding me that "we cannot control what happens to us but we can control our reaction." This book was a constant reminder to seize the day with faith and optimism, regardless of the challenges we faced. It taught us the importance of ruling our attitudes and actions, a lesson that we endeavored to live by and impart to our children and community.

"The Millionaire Real Estate Agent" by Gary Keller was another favorite, especially for me, given my passion for real estate. This book was more than a guide on becoming successful in the real estate industry; it was a roadmap for building a legacy through disciplined work, visionary planning, and unwavering commitment to our goals. Clayton saw in it the blueprint for financial independence and community empowerment, themes that were close to his heart.

Michelle Obama's "The Light We Carry: Overcoming in Uncertain Times" resonated deeply with both of us. Its message of resilience, hope, and the strength found in the community spoke to our core. We were inspired by Michelle's grace and wisdom, seeing parallels in our journey of overcoming obstacles and finding light in the darkest moments. This book encouraged us to carry our own light, to be beacons of hope and strength for each other and those around us. Michelle's book always reminded us of our trip to see President Barack Obama become the 44th President of the United States.

In Clay's words...

"When Barack Obama, a Black man, was chosen by the Democratic Party to run for president, I really hoped it would happen while I was still around. A lot of people thought it couldn't happen in this country because of our history of racism. I knew that too, but I kept hoping. It didn't matter to me if Obama wasn't perfect; he had my vote. For too long, we've treated people unfairly just because of their skin color. It's time we recognize that African Americans have just as much right, value, and pride in this country as anyone else.

It seemed like a lot of young white people felt the same and voted for Obama, the "President of change." As the election day got closer, you could feel the excitement growing. Everywhere you looked, there were signs encouraging people to vote. This was all anyone could talk about, especially at the barbershop. I didn't just want to be alive to see it; I wanted to witness it.

After Obama won, I was determined to go to his inauguration. A person from my church who is a travel agent helped me book tickets for me and Lucy, my partner. It was close to Lucy's birthday, and neither of us had been to Washington, D.C., or seen a presidential inauguration. I decided it was worth it, even if we had to put off paying some bills.

We needed to make sure we had warm clothes because it was going to be cold in D.C. Early on January 21, 2009, we left for Washington on a bus from our church. Our first stop was in North Carolina, where we ended up sharing a table with two reporters. It was a special moment for Lucy's birthday.

We barely slept that night because we were so excited for the next day. The next morning, everyone on the bus was buzzing with excitement. When we got to D.C., we all looked for warm drinks, but they didn't stay warm for long. Despite the cold, everyone was eager to find the best spot to watch the inauguration.

Security was tight, and the mall was packed with people. We managed to find a spot where we could warm up and prepare for the ceremony. Even though it was cold and we were far from the stage, just being there was incredible. Seeing Obama, a man with the same skin color as mine, become president was deeply meaningful. It showed me that no matter our background, we can achieve great things. Obama's presidency made me want to encourage others to improve their lives, whether that's through getting a better job, getting educated, or just working harder. The parade and celebrations were fantastic, and it was a day I'll never forget. It was a reminder not to settle for less and to keep striving for better."

In addition to these, "The Invisibles: The Untold Story of African American Slaves in the White House" provided a stark reminder of our history and the resilience of our ancestors. It was a poignant read that deepened our understanding of the struggles and triumphs of African Americans through the ages. This book, in particular, underscored the importance of remembering our past, not just to honor the legacy of those who came before us but to build upon it, to forge a future where such injustices are a distant memory. The fact that we got to witness a Black man become President of the country seemed like justice for those who the capital.

These books, each in their own way, planted seeds of wisdom, hope, and determination in our hearts. They were our companions in the quiet moments, our guides through the challenges, and our inspiration to dream bigger and reach higher. Clayton and I shared many discussions, debates, and reflections on these readings, which not only enriched our minds but also strengthened the bond between us.

Through these books, we learned that knowledge was not just about acquiring information but about understanding the world around us, recognizing our place within it, and taking action to shape it for the better. They taught us that to plant seeds of knowledge was to sow the future—a future we were determined to make bright, not just for ourselves but for our community and generations to come.

I'm filled with gratitude for the legacy Clayton and I have built together. It's a legacy not just of achievements and accolades but of the knowledge shared, the lives touched, and the seeds planted in the hearts and minds of those who will come after us. In this journey of learning and growth, books have been our faithful companions, lighting the way and reminding us of the power of knowledge to change the world.

Learning as a Community

Our belief in the transformative power of education and knowledge sharing wasn't confined to the four walls of our home. Clayton and I, through our lived experiences and the wisdom gleaned from our readings, sought to extend this ethos to the broader community. This wasn't through formal channels or structured programs but in the manner in which we lived our lives and engaged with those around us.

Clayton's ability to use books as a platform for broader discussions found its most fertile ground in our interactions within the community. Whether it was a casual conversation at the local coffee shop or a more profound dialogue during community gatherings, Clayton had a unique talent for introducing book recommendations that could provide clarity or deepen understanding on a myriad of topics.

For instance, during discussions on economic empowerment or the importance of legacy building, Clayton might casually mention "Think and Grow Rich." It wasn't to hold a seminar on the book's principles but to plant a seed, encouraging individuals to seek out knowledge that could transform their perspective on wealth and success. Similarly, in conversations about resilience and personal growth, "The Light We Carry" would surface, not as a book review but as a beacon of hope and strength that could resonate on a personal level.

Our approach to learning as a community was organic, driven by the belief that knowledge is most powerful when shared freely and woven into the fabric of everyday interactions. We saw every conversation as an opportunity to learn from others and to offer insights that could inspire reflection and growth. This reciprocal exchange of ideas and experiences was, for us, the essence of community learning.

It wasn't uncommon for Clayton to be approached by young entrepreneurs or students who had heard him mention a book in passing and were now seeking advice or further recommendations. These moments were a testament to the impact of sharing knowledge in an accessible and relatable manner. Clayton relished these interactions, seeing them as opportunities to mentor and guide, always with humility and a genuine desire to see others succeed.

Through this informal, community-centered approach to learning, Clayton and I hoped to foster a culture of curiosity, empowerment, and mutual support. We believed that by sharing knowledge—not as a commodity but as a gift—we could inspire others to seek their own paths to growth and fulfillment. This belief was rooted in the understanding that education, in all its forms, is a key that unlocks potential, opens doors, and builds bridges.

As I continue this journey without Clayton by my side, I am comforted by the knowledge that the seeds of wisdom we planted together continue to grow. Our discussions, informed by the books we loved and the experiences we shared, have left an indelible mark on our community. They remind me, and all who were touched by Clayton's spirit, that learning is a journey best undertaken together, with open hearts and minds ready to explore the boundless landscapes of knowledge.

Our story, marked by the shared belief in the transformative power of education, is a testament to the enduring spirit of community and the unbreakable bond of shared dreams. Reflecting on the legacy we aspired to create, one rooted in the empowerment of individuals through literacy, I am reminded of the countless conversations, the books that sparked them, and the lives we touched. These experiences, these moments of connection and growth, have solidified my resolve to carry forward the mission Clayton and I held dear.

The path forward is clear, illuminated by the guiding light of our shared vision. It is a path that calls for continued advocacy for literacy, for the creation of spaces where knowledge is freely shared, and for the support of initiatives that empower individuals to reach their full potential. It is a journey that requires the collective effort of our community, a journey that we must embark upon together.

In honor of Clayton's memory and in service to the future we envisioned, I am committed to the following steps:

1. **Expand Access to Books:** Continue to donate books to schools, libraries, and community centers, focusing on titles that inspire, educate, and empower.
2. **Mentorship and Support:** Increase our involvement in mentoring programs, providing guidance and support to young people as they navigate their educational and personal growth journeys.
3. **Community Dialogues:** Foster open dialogues within the community, using books as a platform to discuss important issues, share experiences, and learn from one another.
4. **Literacy Programs:** Support and volunteer for literacy programs, helping to ensure that individuals of all ages have the opportunity to improve their reading and writing skills.
5. **Advocacy:** Advocate for policies and initiatives that promote literacy and education, recognizing these as foundational to individual and community empowerment.

I do so with Clayton's spirit as my guide and the support of our community as my strength. Together, we can continue to build upon the legacy of literacy, creating a brighter, more empowered future for all. This is a call to action, a reminder of the work still to be done, and an invitation to join us in making the vision of a literate, empowered community a reality. Let us move forward with purpose, with love, and with the unwavering belief in the power of education to change the world.

A Legacy of Finishing

Lucy at BCC Graduation
Lucy Desmore

Clayton at Graduation - BCC

4

Challenges and Triumphs: The Stepping Stones

AFFIRMATION:

"In moments of darkness, when the path ahead seems cloaked in uncertainty, remember that it is not the absence of struggle that defines us, but our response to it. We are architects of resilience, builders of a future where every challenge faced is a stepping stone to greater heights. Let us embrace each trial with courage, knowing that within every moment of adversity lies an opportunity for growth, learning, and unparalleled triumph. Together, with hearts fortified by past struggles and eyes set on the horizon of possibility, we shall continue to pave the path of resilience, leaving a legacy of strength and perseverance for generations to come."

The Blueprint of Resilience

Martin Luther King Jr.'s words, "The ultimate measure of a man is not where he stands in moments of comfort and convenience, but where he stands at times of challenge and controversy," have always echoed profoundly within me, especially during the tumultuous times of life. "Challenges and Triumphs: The Stepping Stones," is a testament to the resilience that Clayton and I, alongside our community, demonstrated in the face of adversity.

Resilience, as we've come to understand it, is not merely the ability to bounce back from setbacks; it's about forging ahead with a renewed sense of purpose, stronger and more determined than before. Our story of resilience during the recession is a reflection of this belief, a narrative woven with the threads of perseverance, faith, and unyielding support for each other.

Drawing parallels with the enduring spirit of the characters in "Remember the Titans" and the profound journey of Booker T. Washington in "Up from Slavery," our experience during the recession was a pivotal chapter in our lives. It was a period marked by significant challenges, yet it was also filled with lessons of hope, strength, and the power of unity.

The recession hit us hard, as it did many families across the nation, particularly within the Black community. The collapse of banks, the crumbling of mortgage companies, and the widespread loss of homes created a storm of uncertainty and despair. Yet, it was in the eye of this storm that Clayton and I found our strength.

As a real estate broker, I was at the frontline of this crisis, witnessing firsthand the devastation it brought to our community and our own doorstep. The impact was immediate and severe, with properties losing value overnight and families finding themselves trapped in untenable financial situations. It was a time when the very foundation of our livelihood seemed to crumble beneath us.

But resilience is built on the bedrock of faith and unity. Clayton and I pulled together, tapping into our savings, including our 401(k)s, to keep our household afloat. It was a humbling experience, one that tested our resolve and our commitment to each other and our careers.

I diversified my efforts, taking on additional jobs, from telemarketing to working at a nursing facility, ensuring that we could meet our obligations and maintain the semblance of normalcy we were accustomed to. Meanwhile, Clayton stood unwaveringly by my side, his belief in me and our future unshaken. He encouraged me to persevere in my real estate career, despite the challenges, and to see this setback not as a defeat but as an opportunity to grow and learn.

This chapter is not just our story but a reflection of the broader narrative of resilience within the Black community during the 2008 financial crisis. It's a story of how, against all odds, we found ways to adapt, to support one another, and to emerge from the crisis with a deeper understanding of what it means to be resilient.

As we delve into the "Blueprint of Resilience," we'll explore the tests of time, share stories of resilience, outline strategies for overcoming adversity, and reflect on the resilient legacy we hope to leave behind.

The Test of Time

The recession that gripped the world in 2008 was more than an economic downturn; it was a crucible that tested the mettle of individuals and communities alike. For Clayton and me, it was a period that challenged every belief we held about security, success, and the American dream. Yet, it was also a time that demonstrated the enduring strength of the human spirit, particularly within the resilient fabric of Black communities.

Facing the Storm Together: As the real estate market plummeted, we found ourselves in the eye of an unforgiving storm. Properties once brimming with value were suddenly underwater, and the once-bustling streets of our community were lined with 'For Sale' signs, symbols of dreams deferred. The impact was not just financial; it was deeply personal. Homes represented more than investments; they were sanctuaries of hope and memories, now threatened by the harsh realities of a market in free fall.

Clayton's unwavering support during this time became my beacon of hope. We pooled every resource available, drawing on our 401(k)s—a decision fraught with its own anxieties but necessary to navigate the immediate crisis. This act of unity, of shared sacrifice, was a testament to our partnership and our determination to withstand the tempest together.

Adaptation and Resilience: My journey through the recession was marked by adaptation. Real estate, the profession I had devoted my life to, was at a standstill. Properties were being stripped bare, not just of their physical attributes but of their potential to provide shelter and security. The emergence of short sales, a term that became synonymous with the crisis, required patience and tenacity. Months of waiting for bank approvals became the norm, each day a test of resilience.

In addition to navigating the tumultuous real estate landscape, I took on various roles outside my chosen profession. From telemarketing to weekend work at a nursing facility, each job was a step toward maintaining our household. These were not just jobs; they were lessons in humility and perseverance, reminders of the importance of doing whatever it took to survive.

The recession, while a time of challenge, also revealed the strength of our community. The economic resilience shown by Black businesses post-recession, the rates of recovery, though slow, were a testament to the collective will to rise above adversity. Our story is but one of many, a narrative shared by countless families who faced the recession's wrath yet refused to be defined by it.

In the face of economic uncertainty, our community rallied together, supporting one another through acts of kindness and solidarity. It was a time that underscored the importance of collective resilience, of finding strength in unity, and of never losing sight of hope. Lessons Learned: The recession taught us invaluable lessons about the nature of resilience. It showed us that resilience is not just about surviving; it's about thriving in the face of adversity. It's about the ability to adapt, to find new paths, and to emerge stronger, with a renewed sense of purpose and determination.

As we navigated through the recession, Clayton and I learned that the true measure of success was not just in weathering the storm but in using the experience as a stepping stone for growth and renewal. Our journey through this period was a testament to our resilience, a blueprint for overcoming challenges that we hoped to pass on as a legacy of strength and perseverance.

Stories of Resilience

In the darkest moments of the recession, when the shadows of doubt and fear loomed large, the stories of resilience from within our community and beyond served as beacons of light, guiding us through the uncertainty. These narratives, each unique in its contours, were united by a common thread—the indomitable spirit of human resilience. As Clayton and I navigated our own trials, we drew strength and inspiration from these tales of perseverance and triumph.

Among the many stories that resonated with us was that of a local entrepreneur who, faced with the closure of his business, transformed his hardship into an opportunity for innovation. With the doors to his physical store shuttered, he ventured into the digital world, creating an online platform that not only revived his business but also provided a lifeline to others in the community. This story was a testament to the power of adaptability and the potential of technology to open new avenues for growth, even in the bleakest of times.

Another narrative that captured our hearts was that of a neighborhood that came together to support families affected by the crisis. With many facing the loss of their homes and livelihoods, the community organized fundraisers, food drives, and skill-sharing workshops. These acts of solidarity were reminders that resilience is not just an individual endeavor but a collective one, where the strength of the community amplifies the resilience of its members.

The story of a fellow real estate agent, who faced bankruptcy and the brink of despair, yet refused to give up on her dreams, was particularly inspiring. Through sheer determination and creative problem-solving, she reinvented her approach to real estate, focusing on affordable housing solutions and community development projects. Her journey from the ashes of financial ruin to becoming a pillar in the reconstruction of her community underscored the belief that from adversity can come strength, innovation, and a renewed sense of purpose.

In the realm of education, teachers and students faced unprecedented challenges as schools closed and learning shifted online. Yet, the resilience shown by educators who adapted to these changes, often with limited resources, was a beacon of hope. They created engaging online curriculums, bridged the digital divide with innovative solutions, and maintained the continuity of education, proving that the pursuit of knowledge could withstand even the toughest of circumstances.

Amidst these stories, Clayton and I found our own path to resilience. The real estate recession had left us reeling, but together, we found ways to adapt and persevere. Clayton's unwavering support as I navigated short sales and sought additional income streams was the foundation upon which we built our resilience. Our story, like many others, was one of facing the unknown with courage, of finding light in the darkness, and of emerging stronger, bound by the conviction that together, we could overcome any obstacle.

These stories of resilience are not just tales of survival; they are blueprints for overcoming challenges, reminders of the strength that lies within and among us. They illustrate the myriad ways in which individuals and communities can rise to meet adversity, transforming challenges into stepping stones toward a brighter future.

As we move forward let's take a look into the practical and aspirational approaches that can guide us through times of trial, drawing on the lessons of resilience that these stories have imparted.

The Resilient Legacy

In the aftermath of the recession, Clayton and I surveyed the landscape of our lives and community, it became evident that the true measure of our journey wasn't found in the obstacles we faced but in the legacy of resilience, we were determined to leave behind. This legacy, shaped by challenges and triumphs, stands as a testament to our collective strength and the enduring power of hope and perseverance.

The most profound aspect of our resilient legacy is the commitment to empowering future generations. Through our experiences, we've learned invaluable lessons about the importance of adaptability, financial wisdom, community support, and the never-ending pursuit of knowledge. These lessons, woven into the fabric of our narrative, are gifts we aim to pass down, ensuring that the next generation is equipped with the tools to navigate their challenges.

Our journey through adversity underscored the pivotal role of community in fostering resilience. We moved forward, our focus remained on strengthening these communal bonds, creating support networks that can withstand economic downturns, and fostering an environment where mutual aid and cooperation were and still are our foundational values. The resilient legacy we aspire to is one where communities are not just surviving but thriving, empowered by a shared sense of purpose and unity.

Central to our resilient legacy is the advocacy for economic empowerment, especially within Black communities disproportionately affected by economic crises. By sharing our story and participating in dialogues around financial education, housing stability, and entrepreneurship, we hope to inspire action and change that lead to greater economic resilience and equity.

Clayton and I have always believed in the transformative power of maintaining a positive outlook. This mindset, cultivated through the trials of the recession, has become a cornerstone of our resilient legacy. It's a reminder that, even in the face of adversity, hope is a choice and a powerful catalyst for change. Our legacy aims to inspire others to view challenges not as insurmountable barriers but as opportunities for growth and renewal.

At the heart of our resilient legacy is the story of our partnership, a testament to the strength found in love and mutual support. Our journey has shown us that resilience is not a solitary endeavor but a shared journey. As we look to the future, our legacy is one of companionship and unwavering support, serving as a beacon for others navigating their paths through adversity.

It's clear that the blueprint of resilience we've crafted is not just for ourselves but for all who seek to overcome adversity. This legacy, built on the foundations of empowerment, community, optimism, and support, is our contribution to the narrative of human resilience—a narrative that continues to evolve with each challenge faced and triumph achieved.

In sharing our story, Clayton and I hoped to light the way for others, offering insights and strategies that can guide them through their times of trial. The resilient legacy we have created is a mosaic of our experiences, a reflection of our belief in the enduring strength of the human spirit, and a call to action for future generations to build upon the lessons of resilience we've learned. I am guided by what Clayton started and determined that his hopes and dreams for a better future for this generation are shared.

The Journey

5

The Harmony of Love and Loss

AFFIRMATION

"I embrace the journey of love and loss with courage and an open heart, carrying forward the legacy of those who have touched my soul deeply. I honor their memory by living with love, kindness, and gratitude, recognizing that their spirit and teachings are forever woven into the fabric of my being. Through every step, every challenge, and every joy, I am guided by their love, finding strength in the memories we shared and the impact they've left on my life. I am committed to sharing this love, to lighting the way for others, and to building a legacy of compassion and resilience that transcends time."

ECHOES OF CLAYTON: THE SYMPHONY OF SORROW AND STRENGTH

Losing Clayton was the hardest thing I've ever faced. Imagine, one day you're planning your future together, and the next, you're trying to figure out how to say goodbye. Helen Keller once said, "What we have once enjoyed deeply we can never lose. All that we love deeply becomes a part of us." These words have become a quiet whisper of comfort in my journey through loss, reminding me that Clayton's spirit, his love, and the life we shared are forever a part of me.

My journey through grief mirrors the story Joan Didion tells in "The Year of Magical Thinking," where she navigates the confusing waves of loss after her husband's sudden death. Like Didion, I found myself in a haze, half-expecting Clayton to walk back through our door, to laugh, to speak, to be the partner I've known and loved.

The movie "Collateral Beauty" touches on something similar, showing how love, time, and even death weave together, shaping our lives in ways we can't always understand. It's about finding beauty in the pain, seeing how our losses connect us, and learning to live with the love that remains.

The night Clayton passed away, I felt numb. Walking out of his hospital room for the last time, and driving home in the silence of the early morning, I was overwhelmed by a sense of unreality. Clayton, my rock, my love, had left this world at 12:27 a.m. on July 22nd, leaving behind a silence that was deafening.

Our house, once filled with his presence, felt strangely quiet, as if it too was mourning. The call from the funeral home at 5:00 a.m. was a stark reminder that this was real. Making arrangements, and choosing a funeral director familiar with Clayton's childhood, felt like moving through a dream I couldn't wake up from.

Clayton's son, my children, our grandchildren... We were all united in our grief, struggling to grasp the reality that Clayton was gone. Each of us, in our own way, tried to find solace in the memories we shared, in the love that Clayton left us with.

I've found myself talking to Clayton's phone, keeping it on as if he might still reach out, a coping mechanism that might seem odd to some but has become a source of comfort to me. It's in these small things, these moments of connection to Clayton's memory, that I find the strength to face each day.

As I write this, sharing our story, I'm reminded of the lessons Clayton taught me about love, resilience, and the beauty that can be found even in our deepest sorrow. This chapter is a tribute to him, to the journey we shared, and to the enduring power of love to bring light into the darkest moments.

THE STAGES OF GRIEF

When Clayton passed away, it felt like I was thrown into a stormy sea of emotions, each wave crashing over me with a different intensity. I've learned that grief doesn't come in neat stages. It's messy, unpredictable, and deeply personal. But understanding that there are common experiences in this journey has helped me feel less alone.

In the days after Clayton's passing, I found myself in disbelief. It was easier to pretend he was still on a trip and would walk through the door any moment. This denial wasn't just a refusal to accept the truth; it was my mind's way of protecting my heart from the full impact of my loss.

Anger came next, a fiery response to the unfairness of it all. Why Clayton? Why now? I was angry at the world, at the illness that took him from us, and sometimes, irrationally, at Clayton himself for leaving. This anger was a sign of the deep love I had for him, a love that felt lost without its rightful home.

Bargaining followed, a series of 'what if' and 'if only' thoughts. If only we'd caught the illness sooner, what if we had tried a different treatment... This stage was my attempt to regain control, to find a solution where there was none, and to hope for a different outcome.

Depression was the heaviest stage, a deep sadness that permeated everything. The world seemed less bright without Clayton. I lost interest in the things we used to enjoy together, and there were days when getting out of bed felt like an insurmountable challenge.

I'm learning that acceptance isn't about being okay with Clayton's death; it's about understanding that it's a part of my reality now. Accepting this has allowed me to start remembering Clayton with more love than pain, to cherish the time we had together, and to begin imagining a future where I carry his legacy forward.

Through each stage, I've found strength in memories, in the signs that Clayton's love is still with me, guiding me. This journey through grief has taught me that love doesn't end with death. It transforms, becomes a part of us, and leads us to find a new way to live with our loss.

FINDING STRENGTH IN MEMORIES

After Clayton passed, the world felt dimmer, quieter, like a vital piece of my life's melody had fallen silent. Yet, in the quiet, I began to hear something else—echoes of the love and joy we shared, resonating through my grief. These memories are sources of strength and comfort in my heart.

I remember Clayton's laughter, a sound that could light up a room and lift the heaviest spirits. Recalling the times we laughed together—over silly jokes, during cozy nights in, or on our many adventures—

brings a smile through my tears. This laughter, a gift from our past, reminds me of the happiness we were fortunate to share, becoming a beacon of light in my darker days.

Clayton was not just my partner but my greatest teacher. From him, I learned the power of perseverance, the importance of kindness, and the courage to face life's challenges with grace. These lessons, imprinted on my soul, guide me as I navigate life without him by my side. Each memory of Clayton teaching me, either directly through his words or indirectly through his actions, is a step on my path toward healing.

It's the everyday moments with Clayton that I find myself recalling the most. Simple things, like the way he'd make coffee in the morning or how we'd share stories from our day in the evening. These memories, seemingly insignificant at the time, have become treasures. They remind me that love is not just found in grand gestures but in the quiet, ordinary moments that make up a life together.

Clayton and I shared many dreams and made countless plans. While it's painful to know we won't realize all of them together, remembering these conversations fills me with a sense of purpose. It's as if Clayton is still encouraging me to pursue our dreams, to live fully not just for myself but for both of us. These memories spur me on, reminding me that carrying forward our shared hopes is a way to honor his memory.

Perhaps the most powerful memory is the love we shared, a love that transcends the physical separation death imposes. This love, unbroken and unchanged by Clayton's passing, is a source of immense strength. It's a reminder that though Clayton is no longer here in body, the love we shared continues to shape my life, to inspire me to love more deeply, and to live more fully.

Through these memories, I've found not just solace but a wellspring of strength. They remind me that Clayton's spirit, his love, and the life we shared continue to echo around me, guiding me toward a future where sorrow and strength sing in harmony.

CLAYTON'S LASTING IMPACT

Clayton was more than just a person; he was a presence, a force of kindness and strength that touched everyone he knew. His passing left a void, yet it also left behind a legacy so vibrant, so full of love, that it continues to guide us.

Clayton's life was a testament to the values he held dear. His unwavering integrity, his relentless optimism, and his boundless compassion weren't just ideals he strived for; they were the very essence of his being. He lived his life as a beacon of hope, showing us that even in the darkest times, there's light to be found in acts of kindness and understanding.

Within our family, Clayton's impact is immeasurable. He was the heart of our home, the steady hand that guided us through storms. His lessons, often shared over dinner or during long walks, continue to resonate with us. He taught us the importance of honesty, the value of hard work, and the unmatched power of love. His children and grandchildren carry forward his legacy, embodying his virtues in their lives and choices. In them, Clayton's spirit burns bright, a guiding light for generations to come.

Clayton's contributions to our community were both large and small, from organizing food drives to offering a listening ear to those in need. He was active at church, helping with outreach and events. He served as part of the security and leadership of Allen Chapel AME Church with a glad heart and a willing spirit. He believed in the power of community, in the strength that comes from people coming together to support one another. Today, the initiatives he started continue to thrive, a testament to his vision of a world where everyone looks out for each other. His legacy lives on in every life he touched, in every project that benefits from his foresight and dedication.

Perhaps the most profound impact Clayton had is the love he shared, a love so deep and enduring that it continues to envelop us. He showed us that love is not just a feeling but an action, a daily commitment to kindness, understanding, and support. This legacy of love is his greatest gift to us, a reminder that even in his absence, we're never truly apart. His love continues to inspire us to be better, to love more freely, and to make a difference in the lives of those around us. He and I enjoyed our lives together and laughed a lot.

As I reflect on Clayton's lasting impact, I'm reminded that we each have a torch to carry, a light to share with the world. Clayton's torch, fueled by love and compassion, has been passed to us. It's our responsibility, and our privilege, to carry it forward, to illuminate the paths of others as he illuminated ours.

In the quiet moments, when I feel his absence most acutely, I find comfort in the knowledge that Clayton's legacy is not bound by time or space. It's alive in every act of kindness, in every moment of connection, in every heart he touched. His legacy is a call to action, a challenge to live with love and purpose, just as he did. Clayton's lasting impact is a testament to the power of one person to make a difference, to inspire change, and to leave a mark on the hearts of those they've loved."A Legacy of Love"

The most vivid threads of our are those of love—unconditional, enduring, and transformative. As I navigate through the world without him by my side, I find solace and strength in the legacy of love he left behind, a legacy that continues to inspire not just me but all who were touched by his spirit.

Clayton's approach to life was grounded in love. He showed me that love isn't just a feeling but a guiding principle, a way to interact with the world. It's about more than affection—it's about actions, big and small, that uplift and support others. His legacy challenges me to lead with love, to make kindness a habit, and to find joy in the happiness of others.

Our shared memories, rich with laughter, adventures, and moments of quiet understanding, are a testament to the love we shared. These memories are not just echoes of the past but beacons for the future, guiding me toward a life that honors Clayton's memory. They teach me that love, once given, never fades—it transforms, grows, and becomes a source of strength.

Embodying Clayton's legacy of love means finding opportunities to express love in my daily actions. It's in the way I reach out to a friend in need, the time I dedicate to listening, and the effort I put into supporting my family and community. Each act of kindness, each moment of compassion, is a tribute to Clayton's enduring influence.

Clayton's love continues to ripple through the lives of those he touched, inspiring others to live more empathetic and to cherish their relationships. By sharing stories of Clayton's kindness, his unwavering support, and his capacity for love, I hope to inspire others to create their own legacy of love, to make the world a kinder, more loving place.

As I write these words, I make a promise—not just to Clayton, but to myself and to the world—to continue the legacy of love he left behind. This promise is a commitment to live each day with purpose, to love without reservation, and to stitch it all together with threads of kindness that will envelop those around me, just as Clayton's love envelops me.

In embracing Clayton's legacy of love, I find not just a path through grief but a way to celebrate his life and the love we shared. It's a journey that doesn't end with his passing but continues, as vibrant and profound as ever, guiding me toward a future where love remains the strongest force of all.

6

Seeds of Hope: Planting the Future Together

AFFIRMATION:

"Together, we are strong. Together, we are capable. Let us move forward with purpose, planting our future together, one seed of hope at a time. Through every challenge and triumph, together we plant the seeds of a brighter tomorrow, nurturing a legacy of unity, resilience, and endless possibility."

The Garden of Community

In the heart of every community lies a garden of potential, waiting for the seeds of hope to be sown. These seeds, tiny yet tenacious, possess the power to transform barren fields into flourishing landscapes of change and growth. Congressman John Lewis once said, "Nothing can stop the power of a committed and determined people to make a difference in our society. Why? Because human beings are the most dynamic link to the divine on this planet." This quote encapsulates the essence of our journey in this chapter, as we explore the profound impact of unity and collective effort in nurturing the garden of our community.

UNFINISHED CHAPTERS: COMPLETING CLAYTON'S LEGACY

Drawing inspiration from "The Great Debaters," a film that celebrates the strength of voice and conviction in the face of adversity, we embark on a narrative that mirrors our own commitment to social change and empowerment. Just as the debaters in the movie, armed with their words and will, challenge the injustices of their time, we, too, engage in our own forms of debate and dialogue, aiming to uplift and inspire those around us.

Our story intertwines with that of a special school, a beacon of hope within our community, dedicated to supporting young women who, against all odds, strive to continue their education while navigating the challenges of teenage pregnancy. This school stands as a testament to what can be achieved when compassion meets action. My personal connection to this cause runs deep, for I see my younger self in these young women. Like them, I faced the trials of being pregnant in high school, without the support of a program like this. Yet, it was my unwavering determination that propelled me forward, allowing me to graduate with my peers against the societal norms of the time.

Clay and I shared a vision for this school, recognizing its importance as a foundation for building futures and fostering resilience. Our involvement, from donating essential items to participating in mentorship events, reflects our belief in the power of community support. Through this story, we illustrate the value of unity, the impact of shared stories from the community, the importance of nurturing future leaders, and the enduring legacy of togetherness.

We carry with us the lessons of the past and the hopes for the future. We acknowledge the role each of us plays in watering the seeds of hope, ensuring they bloom into opportunities for all. Our journey through "Seeds of Hope: Planting the Future Together" gives reflection, inspiration, and action, as we collectively work towards a brighter, more inclusive future.

The Value of Unity

In the narrative of our lives and the history we create together, unity stands as the cornerstone of lasting change and empowerment. The essence of unity is beautifully illustrated in the allegory of the garden: just as diverse plants come together to form a cohesive, thriving ecosystem, so too do individuals within a community unite to cultivate strength, resilience, and progress.

The power of unity is not just in numbers but in the shared vision and purpose that binds us. It's the understanding that our individual stories are brought together to create a picture of collective hope and determination. This unity is forged in the fires of shared struggles and dreams, much like the characters in "The Great Debaters," who, despite their personal and collective challenges, found strength in their unity of purpose against the adversities they faced.

Our community garden, the school for young girls, exemplifies this unity in action. Here, every stakeholder, from educators to volunteers, from local businesses to the young women themselves, contributes to a shared mission. This mission goes beyond academic achievement; it's about building a supportive network that empowers these young women to see beyond their current circumstances to a future filled with possibility.

This garden of the community doesn't grow overnight. It requires the nurturing hands of many, the patience to weather storms, and the faith to see the potential in every seed—every individual. My story, intertwined with Clay's legacy, is a testament to this. Our dedication to this school and its mission reflects our belief in the transformative power of unity. By coming together, and sharing our resources, knowledge, and time, we plant the seeds of hope and watch as they grow into movements of change.

The stories from this community further illuminate the value of unity. Take, for instance, the annual housing fair we organize. It's not just an event; it's a manifestation of our collective effort to ensure everyone has access to affordable housing. This fair, much like the support we extend to the school, is built on the foundation of unity. It's a clear message that we are stronger together, capable of overcoming even the most daunting challenges.

In our pursuit of unity, we also recognize the importance of celebrating diversity within our community. Each individual brings a unique set of experiences, perspectives, and skills to the table, enriching the collective effort. It's this diversity, embraced within the framework of unity, that allows us to address complex issues from multiple angles, ensuring no one is left behind.

As we reflect on the value of unity, we are reminded of the allegorical garden we tend to every day. This garden thrives not because of any single plant but because of the diversity and unity of all its elements. Our community, too, thrives when we come together, sharing in the responsibility of nurturing our future leaders, supporting each other in times of need, and celebrating our successes as one.

The legacy of togetherness, of which Clay was a pivotal part, continues to guide us. It's a legacy that underscores the belief that together, we can overcome obstacles, build bridges, and create a future where everyone has the opportunity to grow, succeed, and flourish. This chapter of our journey, "The Value of Unity," serves as a reminder of the strength we possess when we stand united, committed to planting and nurturing the seeds of hope for generations to come.

Stories from the Community

In every community, stories act as the lifeblood that circulates wisdom, trials, triumphs, and the shared humanity that binds us. These narratives, rich with the hues of personal experiences, paint a vivid picture of the resilience and spirit that define our collective journey. Like the intricate patterns of imagery used to bring stories to life, our community's tales weave a fabric of solidarity, understanding, and inspiration.

One such narrative that stands out is the story of the school for young girls, which has become a sanctuary of hope and transformation. This institution represents more than just an educational facility; it is a beacon of light for those who have been sidelined by circumstances. The story of this school is a powerful testament to what can be achieved when a community comes together to uplift its most vulnerable members. It is a narrative that resonates deeply with my personal journey, reminding me of the struggles I faced as a young woman, pregnant and uncertain about the future. It is a reminder that with support, determination, and a collective effort, barriers can be broken, and dreams can be realized.

The impact of our community's unity is also vividly illustrated in the annual housing fair, a culmination of efforts by individuals, businesses, and organizations to address the pressing need for affordable housing. This event, much like the allegorical garden, brings together diverse elements of our community, each contributing their part to nurture growth and provide shelter. It is a story of hope, where every hand extended and every resource shared becomes a seed of opportunity for someone in need.

These stories from the community are not just narratives of individual achievements but are emblematic of our collective power to enact change. They remind us of the allegory of the garden, where each plant, regardless of its size or species, plays a crucial role in the ecosystem's health and vibrancy. Similarly, each member of our community, regardless of their background or circumstances, contributes to our collective strength and progress.

As we share these stories, we also recognize the importance of nurturing future leaders, the young minds, and hearts that will carry forward the legacy of unity and resilience. The school for young girls is a fertile ground for such leadership, providing not just education but mentorship, encouragement, and the tools needed for these young women to thrive and contribute to society.

These narratives, rich with the essence of our community's challenges and victories, serve as a powerful reminder of the legacy of togetherness that Clay and I cherished. They underscore the belief that every individual has the potential to contribute to the community's well-being, and together, we can overcome the obstacles that stand in our way.

The stories from our community are a mosaic of life's complexities, joys, and sorrows, each piece essential to the whole. As we continue to share these stories, we do so with the hope that they will inspire others to join in the effort to plant seeds of hope and nurture the garden of community for generations to come.

Nurturing Future Leaders

The essence of a community's vitality and its potential for growth lies in its commitment to nurturing future leaders. These emerging leaders, like saplings in a garden, require the right environment, resources, and care to grow strong and resilient. In our community garden, the school for young girls stands as a pivotal greenhouse where these future leaders are cultivated with love, support, and guidance.

This commitment to nurturing extends beyond the confines of the school, permeating every aspect of our community's fabric. It is a testament to the belief that investing in our youth is investing in the future. Just as allegory can reveal profound truths through simple stories, the journey of each young woman at the school symbolizes the broader journey of our community towards empowerment and legacy building.

The personal story I shared earlier, of overcoming the challenges of teenage pregnancy to graduate with my peers, reflects the power of determination and support. It also underscores the importance of mentorship and guidance. In my journey, mentors played a crucial role, offering wisdom, encouragement, and practical advice that helped me navigate the obstacles I faced. Similarly, the mentorship programs at the school aim to provide these young women with role models who can guide them through their challenges, helping them see the possibilities that lie beyond their current circumstances.

Imagery of the garden comes to life when considering the diverse needs of these young leaders. Just as each plant requires specific conditions to thrive—sunlight, water, soil nutrients—each young person needs tailored support to realize their potential. This includes academic tutoring, life skills workshops, and career guidance, all aimed at equipping them with the tools they need for success.

The stories of these young women, each unique yet interconnected, form a mosaic of hope and resilience. One such story is of a young girl who, through the support of the school and the mentorship program, discovered her passion for science and technology. Her journey from uncertainty to becoming a leader in her community's youth tech initiative illustrates the transformative power of education and support. It is a vivid example of how nurturing future leaders can yield remarkable outcomes, changing not just individual lives but the entire community.

UNFINISHED CHAPTERS: COMPLETING CLAYTON'S LEGACY

The legacy of togetherness that Clay and I envisioned is embodied in these efforts to support and uplift the next generation. It is a legacy that recognizes the value of each individual's contribution to the collective strength and harmony of our community. By fostering an environment where young leaders are encouraged to explore their talents, face their challenges with courage, and embrace their roles as agents of change, we plant the seeds of a brighter, more equitable future.

In nurturing these future leaders, we also instill in them the values of love, faith, and trust in oneself and one another. These principles, anchored in the belief in a higher power and the importance of community, serve as guiding lights on their journey. They learn that wealth is not solely measured in monetary terms but in the richness of relationships, the impact of their actions on their community, and the guiding principles that shape their lives.

As we continue to nurture and support these emerging leaders, we do so with the hope that they will carry forward the torch of change, innovation, and community building. Their successes and challenges will become the new stories of our community, inspiring future generations to plant their own seeds of hope and nurture their gardens of potential.

The Legacy of Togetherness

Reflecting on the legacy of togetherness that Clayton and I nurtured together brings a profound sense of continuity and purpose to my journey. This legacy, woven into the fabric of our lives and community, is more than just a series of actions or commitments. It's a living testament to the power of collective spirit, a beacon guiding me as I navigate the path of building upon Clayton's vision while carving out my own space within this legacy.

Our garden of community, ever-flourishing and vibrant, serves as the perfect metaphor for this journey. Just as diverse elements within a garden work in harmony to create a beautiful and life-sustaining ecosystem, our shared dreams and actions with the community mirrored this interdependence. The garden thrives because of its diversity, each plant contributing its unique strength and beauty, much like the varied voices and hands in our community that come together to support one another.

The essence of togetherness, for Clayton and me, was always about more than just being physically present. It was about being emotionally and spiritually connected, sharing our hopes, dreams, and sometimes our fears, as we worked towards a common goal. It was in the quiet moments, planning our next community project, or in the joyful celebrations of our achievements, that I felt the true strength of our bond.

Even in his absence, the legacy of what we built together continues to guide me. It inspires me to keep moving forward, to keep engaging with our community, and to keep sharing our story. The initiatives we supported, like the school for young girls, stand as a beacon of hope and a testament to what can be achieved when we come together with a shared purpose. My continued involvement in these efforts is not just a tribute to Clayton's memory but a reaffirmation of my own commitment to our community's future.

The stories of resilience, hope, and transformation that emerge from our collective efforts are the seeds of this enduring legacy. They are reminders of the impact of togetherness, of the power of a community united in purpose and action. As I share these stories, I do so to plant seeds of inspiration and courage in the hearts of those who will carry this legacy forward.

Building upon this legacy means making intentional choices that reflect the values Clayton and I held dear. It means creating spaces where every member of our community feels valued, heard, and supported. It's about continuing to fight for equity, justice, and inclusivity, ensuring that our garden remains a place where everyone can flourish.

As I reflect on this journey, I am filled with gratitude for the love, lessons, and legacy Clayton left behind. His spirit, a constant presence in my life, encourages me to embrace the challenges and opportunities that lie ahead. The legacy of togetherness we cherished is now my guiding light, a source of strength as I forge my path, honoring our past while looking toward a future filled with hope and possibility.

In this pursuit, I am reminded that the true beauty of our garden lies not just in its blooms but in its roots—the deep, unseen connections that sustain us through every season. As I continue to nurture these roots, I do so with the knowledge that the legacy of togetherness is our most precious inheritance, a gift that will continue to inspire, unite, and propel our community forward for generations to come.

Planting Our Future Together

The journey of reflection, unity, and legacy that Clayton and I embarked upon together continues to unfold in new and meaningful ways. Through the shared stories, the nurturing of future leaders, and the celebration of our community's collective strength, a roadmap for building upon this legacy has emerged. It's a path marked by love, faith, trust in oneself, and in the power of our collective efforts.

"Seeds of Hope: Planting the Future Together" is not just a narrative; it's a call to action—a reminder that each of us has a role to play in the garden of our community. The lessons learned from Clayton's insights, the power of community connections, and the importance of building from the ground up are guideposts for us as we continue to cultivate a legacy that transcends time and circumstance.

The legacy of togetherness that Clayton and I cherished, and which I now carry forward, is a testament to the belief that together, we can overcome any challenge and achieve remarkable things. It's about more than just remembering what was; it's about envisioning and working towards what can be. This legacy is our shared dream, one that we plant and nurture together, ensuring that the fruits of our labor bring joy, inspiration, and opportunity to generations to come.

As we look to the future, let us take the lessons of this chapter to heart. Let us commit to being active participants in the growth of our community, to sharing our stories and wisdom, and to supporting one another in our pursuits. Let us remember that the legacy we build today becomes the heritage of tomorrow.

To honor Clayton's memory and to continue the work we began together, I invite you to join me in this endeavor. Let us each find ways, big and small, to contribute to the flourishing of our community garden. Whether through mentorship, community service, or simply by offering kindness and support to those around us, each action we take plants a seed of hope and possibility.

We Remember - Veterans Memorial

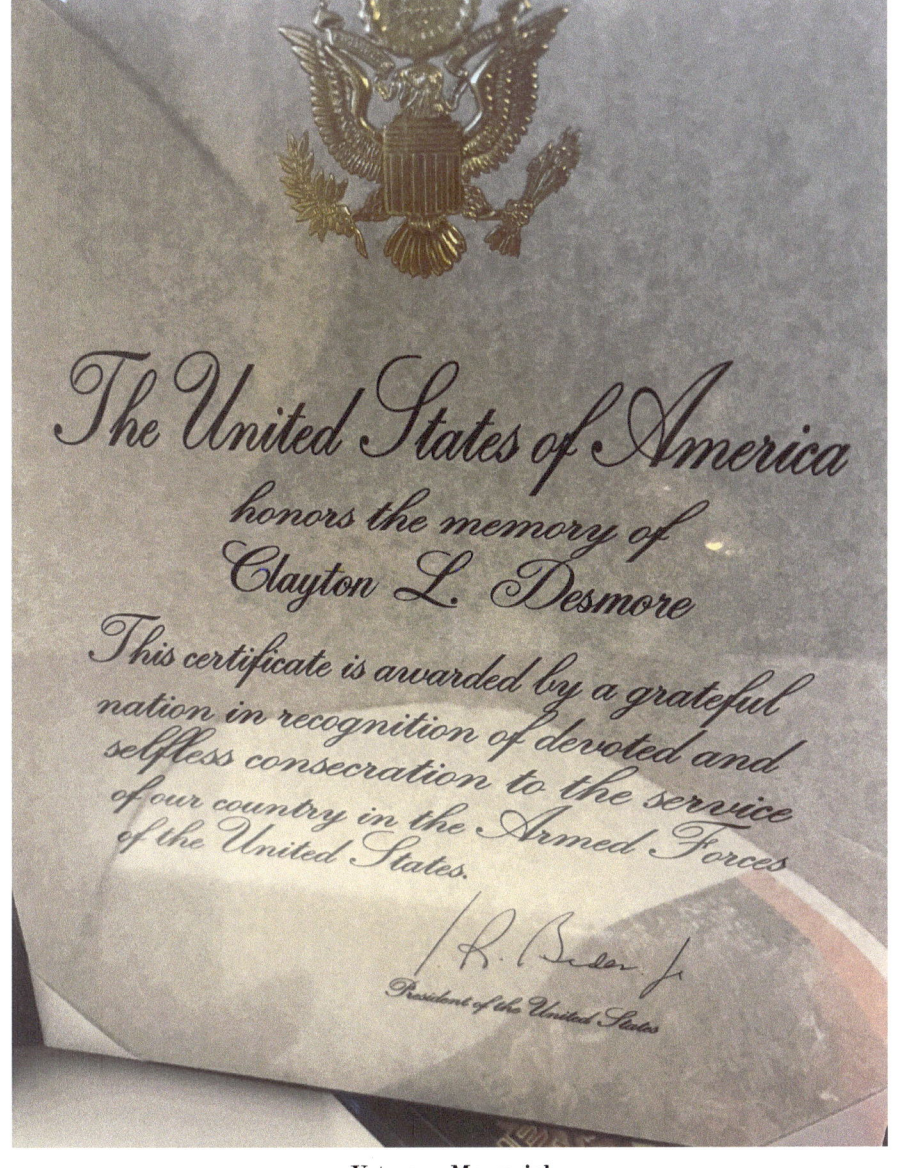

Veterans Memorial
Lucy Desmore

7

Exploring Ancestral Wisdom: Journey to the Roots

AFFIRMATION:

"I stand on the shoulders of giants, my ancestors, whose strength, resilience, and wisdom flow through my veins. I honor their journey by embracing my heritage, understanding that my roots run deep into the rich soil of history and culture. With each step I take on this voyage of discovery, I affirm my connection to the past, drawing strength from the stories of those who came before me. I am a living testament to their endurance and hope, committed to preserving their legacy and passing on their teachings. In my quest for identity, I find not just my story, but the collective narrative of my people, proof of courage, love, and the unwavering spirit to thrive. I am because they were, and in their memory, I continue to grow, learn, and thrive."

The Voyage of Discovery

Alex Haley once said, "In all of us there is a hunger, marrow-deep, to know our heritage - to know who we are and where we came from." This profound hunger, this quest for identity and understanding, sets the stage for our journey in this chapter. As we delve into "Exploring Ancestral Wisdom: Journey to the Roots," we embark on a voyage not just through history, but through the soul-stirring narratives that connect us to our past, illuminate our present, and inspire our future.

The journey to discover our roots is a profound quest for identity, a search that goes beyond mere names and dates to touch the very essence of who we are. This quest is driven by a deep-seated desire to connect with our ancestors, to understand their lives, struggles, and triumphs, and in doing so, to better understand ourselves. It's a journey that, for many of us, is both personal and communal, offering insights not just into our individual pasts but into the shared experiences that unite us as a people.

The significance of this quest was brought into sharp focus for me as I embarked on my own journey to trace my family's lineage and heritage. Growing up, I was surrounded by stories of strong, resilient women and men who, against all odds, carved out spaces of ownership, enterprise, and dignity for themselves. These stories passed down through generations, were not just tales of the past; they were lessons in courage, determination, and the indomitable spirit of my ancestors.

One figure who looms large in my family's history is my uncle, a man whose life story reads like a chapter from Alex Haley's "Roots." Born in the late 1800s in the backwoods of Georgia, he was a testament to what it meant to own one's identity and heritage. Despite the challenges of his time, he managed to secure ownership of vast lands, becoming a respected farmer and businessman in a community where respect had to be earned, especially by a Black man. His achievements were not just personal victories; they were beacons of hope and possibility for the entire community, black or white.

UNFINISHED CHAPTERS: COMPLETING CLAYTON'S LEGACY

The more I learned about my uncle, the more I understood the importance of knowing where we come from. His life was a powerful reminder that our ancestors were not mere footnotes in history; they were architects of their destiny, shaping their future with every decision they made. This realization filled me with a sense of pride and purpose, reinforcing my belief in the power of our heritage to inspire and guide us.

The quest for identity, however, is not without its challenges. For many African Americans, tracing our ancestry can be a daunting task. The legacy of slavery, with its dehumanizing attempt to erase personal histories and familial bonds, has left deep scars, making it difficult for descendants to piece together their lineage. Despite these obstacles, the hunger to know our heritage remains undiminished. Statistics reveal that a significant number of Black Americans are actively seeking to connect with their roots, using a variety of methods from speaking to relatives, conducting online research, to utilizing mail-in DNA services. This search is a testament to our collective resilience and determination to reclaim our stories and identities.

My journey into the world of real estate, which began on the very land my parents owned, was, in many ways, a continuation of my family's legacy of ownership and self-determination. It was a tangible connection to my ancestors, a way to honor their struggles and achievements by building upon the foundation they laid. This journey was not just about property or business; it was about embracing the strength that resides within our DNA, the strength that has been passed down through generations.

As we navigate the quest for identity, we are reminded that knowing our roots is more than an exercise in historical research; it's an exploration of the soul. It's about uncovering the stories of those who came before us, understanding their dreams, their fears, and their hopes, and recognizing how their lives have shaped our own. It's about acknowledging that we are the culmination of their experiences, their resilience, and their spirit.

This quest for identity is a voyage of discovery, one that takes us back to our roots and propels us forward with a deeper sense of who we are and where we belong. It's a journey that reaffirms the belief that there are no limitations except those we place on ourselves. As we explore the ancestral wisdom that lies waiting to be uncovered, let us move forward with the knowledge that our heritage is a source of strength, empowerment, and endless inspiration.

Lessons from the Past

Embarking on a journey to discover our ancestral roots often uncovers more than just names and places; it reveals lessons from the past that resonate deeply with our present and future. These lessons, steeped in the struggles and triumphs of our forebears, offer us invaluable insights into resilience, identity, and the power of legacy. As we delve into the stories of those who came before us, we find not just historical facts but rich experiences that can guide and inspire our own paths.

My exploration into my family's history, particularly the remarkable life of my uncle in Georgia, brought to light the enduring strength and wisdom that has been passed down through generations. His story, emblematic of the broader African American experience, teaches us about the importance of ownership—of land, of identity, and of our narratives. In an era when African Americans were systematically denied the rights to their own stories and futures, my uncle's achievements stand as a testament to the indomitable spirit of those who refused to be defined by the limitations imposed upon them.

This lesson of ownership and self-determination is particularly poignant when we consider the historical context of our ancestors' lives. The legacy of slavery, segregation, and systemic inequality has left scars that still mark the fabric of our society. Yet, despite these barriers, our ancestors carved out spaces for themselves, building businesses, acquiring land, and establishing communities that thrived against the odds. Their lives remind us that our heritage is one of resilience and agency, a legacy of people who, even in the face of unimaginable adversity, never lost sight of their humanity and their right to self-determination.

The story of Solomon Northup, as depicted in "12 Years a Slave," offers another powerful lesson from the past. Northup's resilience in the face of brutal oppression and his unwavering hope for freedom highlight the incredible strength of the human spirit. His journey from freedom to enslavement and back again is a poignant reminder of the fragility of freedom and the importance of fighting to preserve and protect it for ourselves and future generations. It underscores the value of hope, faith, and the belief in the possibility of redemption and justice.

These historical narratives also teach us about the power of community and solidarity. Just as my uncle was respected and supported by his community, and just as Northup's eventual freedom was secured through the efforts of allies and advocates, we are reminded that our struggles and successes are shared. The bonds of community and mutual support have always been vital to African American resilience and progress. Our ancestors knew that strength lies not just in individual achievement but in our collective efforts to uplift and support one another.

Moreover, the lessons from the past encourage us to embrace our identities and the richness of our cultural heritage. In a world that often seeks to marginalize and silence diverse voices, reclaiming and celebrating our ancestry is an act of resistance and empowerment. It's a way to honor those who came before us and to ensure that their stories, sacrifices, and achievements are remembered and cherished.

As I reflect on these lessons from the past, I recognize that they are not just historical artifacts but living principles that can guide us in our own lives. They encourage us to pursue our dreams with determination and courage, to stand firm in the face of adversity, and to build communities that are inclusive, supportive, and strong. By connecting the dots between our past, present, and future, we honor the legacy of our ancestors and commit ourselves to continuing their journey toward freedom, justice, and equality.

Connecting the Dots

In our quest to unearth the roots of our ancestry, we engage in a meticulous process of connecting dots across time and space, weaving together the disparate threads of our history into a coherent narrative. This endeavor is not merely academic; it is an emotional and spiritual journey that reconnects us with our lineage, granting us a deeper understanding of our place in the continuum of history.

The significance of this journey became even more poignant to me as I delved into my own family's past, tracing the lineage of strong women and men whose lives painted a vivid picture of resilience, entrepreneurship, and ownership. My uncle, with his vast lands in Georgia and his revered status in the community, emerged as a beacon of what it meant to claim one's identity and heritage in a time and place that often sought to deny them.

This process of connecting the dots is akin to assembling a puzzle where each piece represents a story, a place, or a moment in time. It involves speaking to elders, sifting through archives, and, in our modern age, utilizing online resources and DNA testing to uncover the layers of our past. The statistics reveal a growing interest among

African Americans in piecing together their family histories, and overcoming the barriers erected by the legacy of slavery and segregation to forge a link to their ancestral past.

The resilience of Solomon Northup, as depicted in "12 Years a Slave," serves as a powerful allegory for this journey. Northup's unwavering determination to reclaim his freedom, despite the brutal attempts to strip him of his identity, mirrors the resolve of countless African Americans seeking to reconstruct their family histories. His story is a testament to the strength of the human spirit, a reminder that even in the face of seemingly insurmountable odds, hope and perseverance can guide us back to ourselves.

In connecting the dots of our ancestry, we do more than just fill in the gaps of our family tree; we reclaim the narratives that have been lost, distorted, or forgotten over time. We honor the struggles and celebrate the achievements of those who came before us, drawing strength from their resilience. This journey allows us to see ourselves as part of a larger story, one that encompasses the pain of loss and separation but also the triumph of survival and legacy.

The lessons gleaned from this endeavor are manifold. They teach us about the importance of knowing our history, not just for the sake of knowledge but for the wisdom it imparts. Our ancestors' experiences, their victories and setbacks, offer valuable insights into the challenges we face today, providing a roadmap for navigating the complexities of identity, belonging, and community in the modern world.

Moreover, this journey of discovery deepens our connection to our culture and heritage, grounding us in a sense of identity that transcends the individual. It fosters a sense of pride in our roots and a commitment to preserving and passing down this rich heritage to future generations. As we connect the dots of our ancestry, it allows us to celebrate the diversity and richness of the African American experience, showcasing the enduring power of family, community, and heritage.

In embracing our roots, we also open ourselves to the broader human story, recognizing that our quest for identity and belonging is a universal one. It is a journey that underscores the interconnectedness of all people, bridging divides and fostering a deeper understanding and appreciation of the myriad ways in which our histories intertwine.

As we move forward, let us carry with us the lessons learned from connecting the dots of our past. Let us honor the legacy of those who paved the way, drawing inspiration from their courage and resilience as we forge our path. In doing so, we not only pay tribute to our ancestors but also lay the foundation for a future in which the next generation can proudly claim their heritage and continue the journey of discovery.

Embracing Your Roots - Including Clay's History

In the heart of our exploration into ancestral wisdom lies not only a journey through time and genealogy but also a profound lesson in resilience and identity. Embracing our roots means connecting deeply with the stories of those who came before us, including the struggles and triumphs of navigating life's challenges. For me, this journey is deeply personal and intertwined with the memory of Clay, whose legacy is a beacon guiding my path.

Clay's history, particularly during the segregation of schools, offers a stark reminder of the obstacles our ancestors faced. His experiences during a time when the world was divided by color lines teach us about the courage required to stand firm in one's identity and beliefs. Clay's story is a testament to the enduring spirit of our people, who, despite systemic barriers, continued to strive for education, dignity, and equality.

UNFINISHED CHAPTERS: COMPLETING CLAYTON'S LEGACY

This narrative of resilience is echoed in my family's legacy, from my uncle's success as a respected landowner and businessman in Georgia to the entrepreneurial spirit that has flowed through our bloodlines. Embracing these roots means recognizing the strength, wisdom, and hope passed down through generations. It means understanding that our ancestors' battles for respect, ownership, and identity were not just for their survival but for the foundation upon which we stand today.

Including Clay's history in our story reminds us of the importance of education and the fight for equality that many of our ancestors were involved in. It highlights the progress made and the work still to be done, inspiring us to continue their legacy of perseverance and advocacy. Clay's experiences during segregation underline the value of unity and community in overcoming adversity, lessons that are vital as we navigate the complexities of our current times.

As we embrace our roots, we do so with a commitment to honor the past while forging a future that reflects the best of what we've inherited. This journey is about more than just personal discovery; it's about paying tribute to the collective history of our people, a history marked by challenges but also by incredible resilience and achievements.

Journey to the Roots: Embracing Ancestral Wisdom

Reflecting on our journey to the roots, we find ourselves at the confluence of the past, present, and future. This exploration has been an enlightening voyage back in time, guided by the stories of our ancestors and the enduring legacy of figures like Clay, whose life during times of segregation offers profound lessons in resilience and determination.

Our exploration into ancestral wisdom, underscored by the narrative of "12 Years a Slave" and the personal stories of my family, has illuminated the path of understanding who we are and where we come from. It has shown us that embracing our roots is a powerful act of self-discovery that connects us with the strength, courage, and hope of those who came before us.

We recognize the importance of remembering and honoring their struggles, celebrating their achievements, and continuing their legacy of resilience. By connecting with our heritage, we ground ourselves in a sense of identity that empowers us to face the future with confidence and purpose.

Let us move forward with the marrow-deep knowledge of our heritage, inspired by the stories of mine and Clay's ancestors. Let us embrace our roots with pride, drawing strength from our history as we navigate the challenges and opportunities ahead. In doing so, we honor the legacy of those who paved the way, ensuring that their spirit lives on in our actions and aspirations.

Our journey to the roots, while concluded in this chapter, continues in our hearts and minds as an ongoing voyage of discovery. It is a journey that strengthens our connection to our past, enriches our present, and inspires our future, reminding us that we are the culmination of our ancestors' dreams and the guardians of their legacy.

Community Recognition

FRESH Books Festival 2023
Lucy Desmore

Hometown Hero
Lucy Desmore

8

The Currency of Knowledge

AFFIRMATION:

"I am a beacon of knowledge and empowerment. Every step I take in my educational journey plants seeds of opportunity, not just for myself but for my community. I embrace the power of learning as a path to freedom, understanding that education is more than knowledge—it's a legacy of strength, resilience, and unity. Through wisdom, I build bridges across generations, lighting the way for those who follow."

The Foundation of Our Future

The founder of Black History Month was Carter G. Woodson. In his book "The Mis-Education of the Negro," I'm reminded of the depth of Clayton's passion for education and his unyielding belief in its power to transform lives. Woodson's words resonate with me, echoing the principles that Clayton lived by and aspired to instill in others. Education, as Woodson articulated, is more than the acquisition of knowledge—it's the key to unlocking our true potential and challenging the constraints placed upon us by history and society.

This journey of understanding and empowerment that Clayton embarked upon mirrors the transformative arc of "Lean on Me," a film that captured the essence of what one person's dedication to change can achieve. Joe Clark, much like Clayton, was a beacon of hope in a system that too often failed those it was meant to uplift. Clayton's story, while uniquely his own, shares this universal theme of resilience, dedication, and the indomitable spirit to effect change.

Clayton's commitment to the youth of our community was profound. He saw in them what many couldn't—a promise of a brighter future, a latent potential waiting to be nurtured. He dedicated himself tirelessly to this cause, engaging with schools, mentoring one-on-one, and even navigating the complexities of the judicial system to advocate for young men who needed guidance the most. His efforts were a testament to his belief in the transformative power of personal attention and education.

Our shared dream was always to empower our children and those around us with the knowledge and wisdom to build a legacy that transcends time and circumstance. Clayton believed, as do I, that education is the cornerstone of this legacy. It's not merely about academic achievement but about fostering a sense of identity, purpose, and connection to a larger community and history.

"Investing in Minds: The Wealth of Education," is both a tribute to Clayton's vision and a call to action. It is an exploration of education's role in shaping futures, building communities, and creating legacies that endure. Through the lens of our shared experiences and the broader challenges and triumphs of our community, we will take a closer look at some specific areas of interest.

- The Power of Education: A reflection on education as a fundamental right and a pillar of empowerment.
- Mentors and Role Models: Celebrating the unsung heroes like Clayton, whose guidance lights the path for others.
- Breaking Barriers: Confronting the systemic challenges that hinder access to education and opportunity.
- A Legacy of Learning: The enduring impact of our efforts and the promise of a brighter future through education.

Clayton's legacy is not just in the lives he touched directly but in the ripple effect of those inspired by his example. As we embark on this chapter, let us honor his memory by recommitting ourselves to the pursuit of knowledge, not just as a personal achievement but as a communal responsibility. Together, we can build a legacy that reflects our highest ideals and aspirations.

The Power of Education

Reflecting on Clayton's vision, I'm drawn back to countless evenings spent discussing the role of education in shaping the destiny of our community. For Clayton, education was never just about reading, writing, or arithmetic; it was about awakening a sense of purpose, identity, and possibility in every young mind he encountered. "Education," he would say, "is the most potent weapon we have to change the world."

Clay believed in teaching our children—and any child who would listen—about the giants upon whose shoulders we stand. This belief was rooted in the powerful legacy of our heritage and the boundless potential of our future. His dedication to education was a beacon that drew many to our doorstep. I remember young men from the neighborhood, often labeled as troublemakers or lost causes by others, sitting at our kitchen table, hanging on Clayton's every word. He had a gift for seeing beyond the exterior, recognizing the latent potential within each of them. His mentoring was a blend of tough love and unwavering support, challenging them to strive for excellence and to see education as a ladder to their dreams.

The impact of his work was palpable. I witnessed transformations that seemed nothing short of miraculous. Young men who had once been on a path to nowhere began to talk of college, of careers, of giving back to their community. Clayton's belief in them had lit a spark, revealing the wealth of education in its most profound form—not merely as a path to economic stability but as a journey toward self-discovery and empowerment.

Yet, the challenges were ever-present. The achievement gaps that persisted in our schools were a stark reminder of the systemic barriers facing our children. The statistics were disheartening, showing how racial disparities in education could undermine the potential of so many bright young minds. But Clayton never wavered in his conviction that these barriers could be overcome. He worked tirelessly, advocating for changes in the school system, partnering with educators, and reaching out to community leaders to create a more inclusive and supportive educational environment.

His efforts extended beyond academic support. Clayton understood that true education encompasses the development of the whole person—intellectually, emotionally, and socially. He organized outings and events that taught valuable life skills, from teamwork and communication to leadership and resilience. Through his work, education became a holistic journey of growth, preparing young people not just for the challenges of the classroom, but for the challenges of life.

As I continue this legacy, I am guided by Clayton's unwavering belief in the power of education to transform lives. His vision inspires me to advocate for educational equity, to support mentorship programs, and to continue the fight for a future where every child has the opportunity to realize their full potential. The currency of knowledge, as Clayton so often reminded us, is the foundation upon which we build our dreams.

Mentors and Role Models

Mentors and role models provide strength, color, and direction. Clayton's role as a mentor was a calling he embraced with every fiber of his being. His approach was grounded in the belief that every young person, regardless of their background or the obstacles they faced, deserved someone who believed in them unconditionally.

Clayton often spoke of the mentors who had shaped his own journey—teachers, community leaders, and family members who had seen something in him that he had not yet seen in himself. These were the individuals who had taught him the value of hard work, the importance of integrity, and the power of faith. They were his guiding lights, and in turn, he became a beacon for others.

The role of a mentor, as Clayton practiced it, went far beyond the conventional. It was not merely about providing advice or academic tutoring. It was about building relationships based on trust, respect, and mutual understanding. Clayton knew that to truly impact a young person's life, he had to be present—not just as a teacher, but as a listener, a confidant, and sometimes even a surrogate parent.

His commitment to mentorship was evident in the countless hours he spent with young men in our community. Whether it was through one-on-one mentoring sessions, group discussions, or simply being a consistent presence in their lives, Clayton made it his mission to provide the guidance and support these young people so desperately needed. He understood that the role of a mentor was not to create a mirror image of oneself but to help each individual discover their own unique path to success.

Clayton's mentorship extended to the courtroom, where he often advocated for young men who found themselves entangled in the legal system. He believed in second chances and fought tirelessly to ensure that a mistake did not define a person's entire life. His interventions, including proposals for alternative sentencing like community service or educational programs, reflected his deep conviction that every young person deserved the opportunity to learn from their mistakes and make positive changes in their lives.

The legacy of Clayton's mentorship is a testament to the transformative power of positive role models in the lives of young people. Through his example, he showed that mentorship is about more than just guiding someone on the right path; it's about empowering them to believe in their own potential and to pursue their dreams with courage and determination.

As we reflect on the importance of mentors and role models, we recognize that Clayton's approach to mentorship offers valuable lessons for all of us. It challenges us to ask ourselves how we can be more present in the lives of the young people around us. How can we offer our support, our guidance, and our belief in their potential? In honoring Clayton's legacy, we are reminded that each of us has the capacity to be a mentor, to make a difference in someone's life, and to contribute to the strength and resilience of our community.

In the next section, we will delve into the challenges of breaking barriers within the educational system and society, exploring how we can collectively work to create more inclusive and equitable opportunities for all.

Breaking Barriers

In our journey together, Clayton and I encountered numerous barriers that seemed insurmountable. Yet, his unwavering spirit and dedication to our community's youth taught me an invaluable lesson: barriers are not endpoints, but challenges to be overcome. This belief was at the heart of Clayton's mission to break down the systemic obstacles that hinder the educational success and empowerment of our community.

The disparities in educational outcomes for Black students, as highlighted by the statistics we've discussed, are a stark reminder of the systemic barriers entrenched in our society. These gaps are not just numbers; they represent lost potential, unfulfilled dreams, and the perpetuation of cycles of poverty and disenfranchisement. Clayton understood that to truly make a difference, we needed to address these issues head-on, with a combination of advocacy, direct action, and community mobilization.

One of Clayton's key strategies was to work within the system to create change. He engaged with educators, school administrators, and policymakers, advocating for reforms that would provide more equitable educational opportunities. He pushed for the implementation of culturally relevant curricula, the recruitment and retention of Black teachers, and the development of support programs that addressed the unique needs of Black students.

Clayton also recognized the importance of community involvement in breaking educational barriers. He organized workshops and forums for parents and community members, empowering them with the knowledge and tools to advocate for their children's education. He believed that a united community could wield significant power in demanding and enacting change.

Despite the progress made, Clayton was acutely aware of the ongoing challenges. The achievement gaps might have narrowed, but they remained "very large," a sign that much work was still needed.

He knew that this was not just an educational issue but a societal one, rooted in broader patterns of inequality and discrimination.

Clayton's approach to breaking barriers extended beyond the educational system. He tackled issues of racial profiling, juvenile justice, and economic inequality, understanding that these were all interconnected with the educational disparities our community faced. His work reminded us that to truly empower our youth, we must address the myriad barriers they encounter in their daily lives.

The legacy Clayton left behind is a blueprint for action. It challenges us to continue the work of breaking barriers, not only in education but in all areas of life that impact our community's well-being. It calls on us to be advocates, allies, and activists, to stand up against injustice, and to work tirelessly for a future where every child has the opportunity to succeed, regardless of their background.

As we move forward, let us carry Clayton's legacy with us, inspired by his example to break down the barriers that stand in the way of our collective progress. In the next section, "A Legacy of Learning," we will reflect on the enduring impact of our efforts and the ongoing quest for educational equity and excellence.

A Legacy of Learning

In the echoes of Clayton's footsteps, a path is illuminated—not just for me, but for our entire community. This path, paved with challenges overcome and victories won, leads us toward a legacy of learning. It's a legacy that transcends the confines of classrooms and textbooks, reaching into the heart of what it means to empower and be empowered.

Clayton's vision was clear: education is the cornerstone upon which we build a more equitable, just, and compassionate world. His life's work, dedicated to the youth of our community, was a testament to his belief in the transformative power of knowledge. But more than that, it was a demonstration of his commitment to passing on a legacy of learning that would outlive him.

A legacy of learning is not merely about academic achievement; it's about instilling values, fostering critical thinking, and nurturing a sense of responsibility towards oneself and one's community. Clayton understood this deeply. He saw each act of mentorship, each intervention on behalf of a young person, as a seed planted for the future—a future he believed could be brighter, more inclusive, and more just.

The legacy Clayton leaves behind is one of action and hope. It challenges us to ask: What are we doing to contribute to this legacy? How are we ensuring that the lessons of the past inform the actions of the present and the plans for the future? It's a call to each of us to take up the mantle of mentorship, to advocate for educational equity, and to continue the work of breaking down barriers that limit potential.

Reflecting on Clayton's impact, I am reminded of the countless young lives he touched, many of whom have gone on to achieve great things. Their successes are a living tribute to Clayton's belief in the power of education. But beyond individual achievements, the true measure of his legacy is seen in the continued efforts of our community to value and prioritize learning—in all its forms.

"A Legacy of Learning" serves as both a foundation and a beacon. It is a foundation upon which we build our continued efforts to empower the next generation. It is a beacon that guides us toward a future where every child has access to the opportunities and support they need to thrive.

This legacy is not static; it evolves with each generation, enriched by new knowledge, perspectives, and challenges. It is our responsibility to carry this legacy forward, to adapt it to the needs of the times, and to ensure that it remains a source of strength and inspiration for all who come after us. Together, we can continue to build on Clayton's legacy, creating a future that honors his memory and reflects our highest aspirations.

Building Our Future Together

I reflect on the journey Clayton and I embarked upon—a journey of love, struggle, and unwavering belief in the power of education. Clayton's legacy, etched in the lives he touched and the barriers he broke, offers us a blueprint for action, a roadmap for building a future that honors his vision and our collective aspirations.

As we move forward, let us carry Clayton's legacy with us, not just as a memory but as a call to action. Here are some steps we can take to continue this important work:

- **Engage with Our Community**: Become involved in local education initiatives, mentorship programs, and advocacy efforts to support equitable access to education.
- **Support the Youth**: Look for opportunities to mentor or support young people in your community. Your guidance and belief in their potential can make a significant difference.
- **Advocate for Change**: Use your voice to advocate for educational reforms that address the needs of all students, especially those who are marginalized or underserved.
- **Educate Ourselves and Others**: Continue to learn about the issues facing our education system and share this knowledge with others. Education is a collective journey, and we all have a part to play.

I have a heart full of gratitude for the life and lessons of my beloved Clayton. His dream was for all children to have the opportunity to learn, grow, and succeed. Let us honor his memory by dedicating ourselves to making this dream a reality. Our journey does not end here; it is just the beginning of a collective effort to build a brighter, more equitable future for all. Together, we can create a legacy that transcends generations—a legacy of love, empowerment, and unyielding commitment to the transformative power of education.

Still We Press Forward

We are Overcomers
Bethune Publishing

Family is Everything
Bethune Publishing

9

The Art of Perseverance

AFFIRMATION:

"In my journey, faced with daunting challenges, I stand anchored in the belief that I possess an unwavering spirit of perseverance. Each step and breath is a testament to my resilience, my strength, and my ability to surmount obstacles. Drawing inspiration from the courageous souls before me, their determination, and their faith in unity and action, I realize my path is intertwined with a supportive community. Together, we transform adversity into opportunities for growth, learning, and victory. I cherish the wisdom of our collective experiences, seeing them as milestones towards my potential. Moving forward, I am fueled by the conviction that, despite the odds, my steadfast will shall impact the world significantly. This affirmation, my mantra, underscores my dedication to not just endure but to flourish and contribute to an enduring legacy of empowerment, hope, and boundless possibilities."

Against All Odds: Stories of Resolute Will

Alice Walker once said, "The most common way people give up their power is by thinking they don't have any." This profound statement captures the essence of our narrative in "Against All Odds: Stories of Resolute Will." Our journey—mine and Clayton's—has been one of facing seemingly insurmountable challenges with a spirit of determination that could move mountains.

As I sit here, reflecting on our path, I am reminded of Toni Morrison's "Beloved," a narrative that delves into the depths of human resilience in the face of the unimaginable. Like the characters in Morrison's masterpiece, Clayton and I found strength in our shared history, in the love we had for our community, and in our commitment to justice.

Our story is not unlike the historical march captured in the film "Selma" (2014), where individuals, armed with nothing but their courage and conviction, changed the course of history. It was this spirit of perseverance that Clayton exhibited when he took a stand at his newly integrated school, a microcosm of the larger civil rights movement sweeping across the nation.

The Spirit of Clayton's Stand

In those early days, promises of inclusion and equality were as empty as the classrooms that should have welcomed every student, regardless of color. Clayton, however, saw through the hollow assurances. When the principal, a man who later revealed his allegiance to the Ku Klux Klan, failed to honor his word, Clayton did not falter. He understood, as John Lewis said, the importance of getting into "good trouble."

Lowering the American flag in tribute to Dr. Martin Luther King Jr., Clayton and his fellow students used their trumpets to mourn a hero and to protest the injustice that permeated their lives. It was an act of defiance, but more importantly, an assertion of their dignity and rights. Despite the threats and the suspension that followed, Clayton's actions sparked a movement within the school. His leadership, his unwavering demand for respect, and his ability to inspire solidarity among his peers were a testament to his extraordinary character.

This chapter, "Against All Odds: Stories of Resolute Will," is a tribute to that enduring spirit of perseverance. It's a recognition of the battles fought and won, not with weapons, but with an unbreakable will to demand and enact change. Our narrative is a reminder that the art of perseverance is not merely about surviving; it's about thriving against all odds. It's about how, even in the darkest of times, the human spirit can find a way to shine brightly, guided by the belief in something greater than oneself.

I will never forget that our history, with its trials and triumphs, is a wellspring of strength. It is a story that must be told and retold, for in its telling, we find the courage to face our own challenges and to continue the work that Clayton and so many others continued to do because of the path made for them and the one they were determined to leave for others.

The spirit of endurance is a powerful force, one that has propelled us through times of turmoil and triumph alike. It's a force that was embodied by Clayton in every challenge he faced, every obstacle he overcame. His resilience wasn't just a personal attribute; it was a beacon of hope for our community, a testament to what we can achieve when we stand firm in our convictions.

Reflecting on Clayton's legacy, I am reminded of the countless stories of Black-owned businesses that, despite facing systemic barriers and adversity, have grown and thrived. These entrepreneurs embody the spirit of endurance, demonstrating that with perseverance, innovative thinking, and a deep commitment to community, it's possible to overcome even the most daunting challenges.

Our narrative is rich with testimonies of triumph, stories of individuals and communities that refused to be defined by their circumstances. These stories are not just accounts of survival; they are celebrations of the human spirit's capacity to persevere and to transform adversity into opportunity.

One such story is that of a local business owner, a friend of Clayton's, who started a bookstore in a neighborhood that had no libraries. Faced with skepticism and numerous challenges, including limited access to funding and resources, she persisted. Her bookstore became more than just a place to buy books; it was a community hub, a place where people came together to learn, share, and grow. Her success is a testament to the power of endurance and the impact one person can have on a community.

The Role of Faith and Hope

In our journey, faith and hope have been constant companions, guiding us through the darkest of times. Clayton's faith was not just a source of personal comfort; it was a catalyst for action. It was his faith in a better future that drove him to take a stand at his school, to mentor young people, and to fight for justice.

Hope, too, played a crucial role. Even when faced with seemingly insurmountable obstacles, Clayton never lost hope. He believed in the potential of our community to rise above adversity, to come together in solidarity and support of one another. His hope was contagious, inspiring others to believe in the possibility of change.

As we reflect on the art of perseverance, we recognize that it is more than just a personal attribute; it is a legacy we inherit and pass on. Clayton's story, and the stories of countless others who have faced adversity with courage and determination, are a part of this legacy. Our challenge is to carry forward this legacy of perseverance, to draw strength from

UNFINISHED CHAPTERS: COMPLETING CLAYTON'S LEGACY

the examples set by those who came before us, and to continue their work of building a more just, equitable, and compassionate world. It is a challenge we must embrace with both hands, for in the act of persevering, we honor their memory and contribute to the creation of a future filled with hope and possibility.

In the heart of our struggle lies the strength of our triumphs. Each story of success against the odds is a beacon of light that illuminates the path for those who follow. These testaments are not merely tales of personal achievement but milestones in our collective journey toward empowerment and equality.

Clayton's courage in the face of systemic injustice, particularly during the turbulent times of the Civil Rights Movement, serves as a cornerstone of our discussion on triumph. His decision to lower the American flag in homage to Dr. Martin Luther King Jr., amidst threats and opposition, is a poignant reminder of the sacrifices made for the freedoms we strive to uphold today.

This act of defiance, rooted in a deep respect for justice and equality, inspired a wave of change within his community. Clayton's ability to lead, even when faced with personal risk, encouraged his peers to demand their rightful place in society, setting a precedent for the power of unified action.

The resilience of Black-owned businesses, flourishing despite systemic barriers, mirrors Clayton's indomitable spirit. These enterprises are not just economic ventures; they are pillars of the community, providing services, employment, and a sense of belonging to those they serve. Their success stories are a powerful rebuttal to the narrative of limitation, showcasing the boundless potential of perseverance and entrepreneurial spirit.

One such story is of a local café that became a sanctuary for artists, activists, and community members to gather, share ideas, and support one another. Despite financial hurdles and societal skepticism, the café's founders persisted, driven by a vision of creating a space where culture and community could thrive together. Today, it stands as a testament to their tenacity, a vibrant hub that nourishes both body and soul.

Faith and hope have been the bedrock of our endurance. In moments of doubt and despair, it is our faith in a higher purpose and our hope for a better future that sustains us. These virtues are reflected in the stories of those who, like Clayton, have faced adversity with a steadfast heart.

The role of the community in these triumphs cannot be overstated. It is in the collective strength, the shared struggles, and the mutual support that we find our greatest victories. Each success story is a testament of our community's resilience, woven together by the hands of those who refuse to give up.

As we celebrate these testimonies of triumph, we are reminded of the journey that lies ahead. The road may be fraught with challenges, but it is paved with the victories of those who dared to dream, to fight, and to persevere. Let their stories inspire us to continue the work of building a world that reflects our highest ideals of justice, equality, and community.

In our narratives of perseverance, faith and hope emerge not just as abstract concepts but as tangible forces that drive us forward. These elements have been the bedrock upon which communities facing adversity have built their dreams and visions for a better future. They are the unseen hands that guide us through our darkest hours, reminding us of our strength and the promise of tomorrow.

Faith, in many ways, has been our compass. It's a deep-seated belief in the righteousness of our cause and the knowledge that, despite the hurdles, there is a path to victory. For Clayton and me, faith was not passive; it compelled us to act, to stand up against injustice, and to strive for a community where everyone has the opportunity to thrive.

This action-oriented faith is evident in the movements that have shaped our history. It's seen in the courage of those who marched from Selma to Montgomery, demanding their right to vote. Their journey, steeped in faith, was a powerful assertion of their humanity and their unyielding demand for justice.

Hope plays a complementary role to faith; it is the vision that guides us. It's the light at the end of the tunnel, the belief that no matter how tough the present may seem, the future holds the promise of change. Hope was what Clayton held onto as he navigated the challenges of integrating schools and fighting for equality. It's what kept him going when faced with threats and opposition—not just the hope for his own safety, but for a future where such battles would no longer be necessary.

The resilience of Black-owned businesses, thriving against the odds, is a testament to the power of hope. These entrepreneurs look beyond the immediate challenges, envisioning a future where their ventures not only succeed but also contribute to the economic empowerment of their communities. Their success stories are beacons of hope, showing us what's possible when we dare to dream and work towards those dreams with determination.

For me and Clay, faith and hope have been the anchors that kept us grounded. They were the forces that propelled Clayton to become a beacon of change and have continued to guide me in preserving his legacy. These virtues remind us that our fight is not just for the here and now but for the generations to come. Faith and hope inspired us to build a legacy that transcends our individual lives, creating a foundation of strength, resilience, and possibility for the future.

As I move forward, I hold onto faith and hope, not as mere words, but as principles that animate my actions. I hold on to the fuel that drives me to continue the work that Clayton and so many others have started. In the face of adversity, I will remember that it is faith in a better world and hope for the future that will ultimately lead us to triumph.

The Legacy of Perseverance

The stories I've shared, the battles fought, and the victories won all contribute to a legacy of perseverance that is both a gift and a responsibility. This legacy is not merely about remembering the past; it's about using the history of a strong man, born of a strong people as a foundation upon which to build a future filled with hope, equality, and justice.

The legacy of perseverance is a torch passed down through generations, lit by the courage of those who dared to dream of a better world. It's a legacy that Clayton carried with pride, one that I am committed to continuing in his honor. This legacy calls on us to be agents of change, to use our voices, our actions, and our lives to make a difference in the world around us.

In the spirit of this legacy, we must ask ourselves: How can we contribute to the ongoing fight for justice and equality? How can we ensure that the lessons of the past are not forgotten but are used to illuminate the path forward? The answers to these questions lie in our willingness to engage, to educate, and to empower ourselves and others.

The legacy of perseverance teaches us the power of collective action. It reminds us that while individual efforts are important, it is when we come together as a community that we can effect the most significant change. It's a lesson evident in the civil rights movements, in the resilience of Black-owned businesses, and in the stories of triumph that dot our history.

As we look to the future, let us commit to fostering a sense of unity and purpose. Let's build networks of support that uplift and empower, create spaces for dialogue and understanding, and work together to address the challenges that face our communities. In doing so, we honor the legacy of those who came before us and contribute to a world that reflects our highest ideals.

The legacy of perseverance is a call to action. It urges us to not be complacent, to not accept the status quo if it stands in the way of justice and equality. It challenges us to continue the work started by Clayton and countless others, to strive for a society where every individual has the opportunity to succeed and to be recognized for their inherent worth.

As we close this chapter, let us move forward with a renewed sense of purpose. Let us carry the torch of perseverance with pride, knowing that our actions today are the foundation for tomorrow's achievements. Together, we can continue to break barriers, to build bridges, and to create a legacy of perseverance that will inspire generations to come.

Empowerment

As we reflect on the journey Clayton and I have navigated, marked by resilience, faith, and a steadfast commitment to empowerment, it's clear that our story is not just our own. It's a narrative interwoven with the strength and spirit of those who came before us and those who will follow. This chapter, rooted in our personal and collective struggles against the odds, serves as a testament to the enduring power of will, the importance of community, and the unbreakable bond of shared purpose.

Our legacy, built upon the foundations of perseverance and hope, is a beacon for future generations. It's a legacy that speaks to the essence of human resilience—the ability to face adversity with courage and to emerge not just unscathed but stronger, wiser, and more determined. Clayton's vision and dedication, coupled with our collective efforts, have sown the seeds of empowerment, nurturing a future where obstacles are viewed not as barriers but as opportunities for growth and triumph.

Throughout our journey, the role of our community has been paramount. In times of need, our community stood as a pillar of support, embodying the timeless adage that together, we can achieve the impossible. This collective strength, grounded in empathy, solidarity, and action, has been instrumental in our efforts to uplift, inspire, and effect meaningful change. It's a reminder that no act of kindness, no matter how small, is ever wasted, and that every effort to make a difference counts.

My focus turns to the future and the responsibility of passing the baton to the next generation. It's about ensuring that the lessons learned, the wisdom gained, and the legacy we've built continue to inspire and guide those who will carry forward the torch of empowerment. I am committed to fostering an environment where mentorship, education, and community engagement are valued and prioritized, and where every individual is empowered to reach their full potential.

Our story is a call to action—a reminder that we all have the power to make a difference in our own lives and the lives of others. It's a call to embrace the challenges we face with resilience and hope, to support one another in our endeavors, and to contribute to a legacy of empowerment that will resonate for generations to come. As Clayton and I have learned, against all odds, it's possible to create a ripple of change that grows into a wave of positive impact.

I hope that what I shared will serve as a beacon of hope, a source of inspiration, and a reminder of the power of resolute will. May our story, interwoven with the stories of those around us, continue to inspire courage, foster unity, and ignite a passion for making a difference. Together, we can build a future where empowerment, resilience, and community support are the cornerstones of success and fulfillment.

10

The Harmony of Health and Wealth

AFFIRMATION:

"I affirm my commitment to balancing prosperity with well-being, recognizing health as my most valuable asset. Inspired by Clayton's journey, I pledge to advocate for equitable healthcare, embrace holistic wellness, and nurture the physical, mental, and spiritual health of myself and my community. I am determined to forge a legacy of health and wealth in harmony, ensuring a prosperous future for all."

"Beloved, I pray that you may prosper in all things and be in health, just as your soul prospers." - 3 John 1:2.

This scripture lays the foundation for our exploration into the crucial balance between physical well-being and the pursuit of success. Inspired by Clayton's life journey and informed by the broader narrative of health disparities within the African American community, this chapter seeks to illuminate the path to achieving both health and wealth in harmony.

Remembering Clayton's life, segmented by significant experiences and challenges, I hope to share insights into how his health journey profoundly influenced our shared approach to life, business, and community engagement. From his early life in a family that moved frequently due to segregation, through his service in the Navy, to his professional career and our life together, health remained a central theme.

The Wealth in Health

Drawing on Clayton's narrative and the broader context of African American health disparities, we see the undeniable truth: health is not merely a personal asset but a communal wealth. The disparities in healthcare access and outcomes, particularly for African Americans, underscore the need for a holistic approach to health—one that considers the social, economic, and environmental determinants of health.

Let's explore the holistic concept of health that encompasses mind, body, and spirit, a philosophy increasingly embraced within the African American community. It will interweave personal anecdotes, such as Clayton's health challenges and their impact on our life choices, with an analysis of the systemic issues contributing to health disparities. By maintaining health across all aspects of our being, we can enhance our capacity for resilience, creativity, and sustained success.

Clayton's life, marked by his early experiences, his time in the military exposed to harmful chemicals, and his subsequent health challenges, offers critical lessons on the intersection of health and wealth. His determination to prioritize family, community, and health over material success provides a powerful blueprint for living a balanced and meaningful life. I hope that by sharing a glimpse at Clayton's experiences I shed light on the broader challenges faced by African Americans in the healthcare system and the importance of advocating for equitable healthcare access and outcomes.

Clayton leaves behind a legacy that challenges us to pursue success without sacrificing our well-being. Consider strategies for advocating for healthcare reform, engaging in community health initiatives, and integrating health into our daily lives and ambitions. By striving for a world where health disparities no longer exist, we honor Clayton's memory and contribute to a future where all individuals can achieve both prosperity and wellness.

Clayton and I are rooted in our Christian faith and our commitment to social justice, serves as a call to action. This commitment taught us that is not just material. We learned to view success through a lens that values health as the ultimate wealth, guided by a deep understanding of the challenges and disparities that affect our communities.

In a world where the pursuit of success often overshadows the importance of well-being, Clayton's journey alongside the broader struggles of the African American community remind us of an essential truth: health is the foundation upon which true prosperity is built. The disparities in health outcomes and access to care that disproportionately affect African Americans highlight a crucial gap in our society's understanding of wealth.

The health challenges Clayton faced, exacerbated by a system fraught with inequalities, mirror the broader issues confronting African Americans. Despite advancements in healthcare access through initiatives like the Affordable Care Act, African Americans continue to face higher rates of chronic illness, mortality, and inadequate access to quality care. These disparities are not just numbers; they represent real lives, potential unfulfilled, and families impacted by systemic failings.

Recognizing health as a communal wealth calls for a shift in perspective. It compels us to advocate for a healthcare system that serves all equitably, acknowledging the social determinants of health that include economic status, education, and the environment. The African American community's growing movement toward holistic health emphasizes the interconnectedness of mental, physical, and spiritual well-being, challenging us to consider health in all policies and practices.

Clayton's approach to life, characterized by a deep faith and commitment to community, exemplifies how health and prosperity are intertwined. His insistence on prioritizing well-being, nurturing close family relationships, and making his family a priority despite the challenges he faced, offers a blueprint for balancing prosperity with wellness. In honoring Clayton's legacy, we are called to advocate for a balanced approach to success—one that places health at its core.

As we reflect on the lessons from Clayton's journey and the disparities faced by African Americans, we must engage in collective action to address these inequities. This involves supporting policies that expand healthcare access, promoting community health initiatives, and educating ourselves and others about the importance of holistic well-being.

By embracing health as the true wealth, we honor those who have struggled for access to care and those who continue to face systemic barriers. Our pursuit of prosperity must be rooted in the well-being of all individuals, recognizing that a healthy community is the foundation of a thriving society.

Mind, Body, and Spirit

Being really healthy means taking care of your mind, body, and spirit all together. Our ancestors knew it wasn't enough to just be physically fit; they also made sure to stay close to nature and God. But nowadays, a lot of us have lost this connection, and you can see how it affects many people in the African American community. Thinking about health in this complete way – where your mind, body, and spirit are all connected – is an old idea but it's also super important right now. True health means being good physically, but also feeling good inside your head and heart.

The idea of holistic health is like making sure every part of a plant gets what it needs - water, sunlight, and good soil - so it can grow strong and healthy. It's not just about one person trying to be healthy on their own, but everyone in the community working together, especially in the African American community where unfair treatment and racism have made staying healthy even harder. This whole-community approach to health is about paying attention to our bodies, minds, and spirits all at the same time, kind of like how our grandparents understood the importance of connecting with nature and their faith.

Clayton's story teaches us a lot about why it's important to look after every part of ourselves. When he was in the military, he was around some dangerous chemicals that made him really think about his health in a new way. He showed us that being truly healthy means taking care of our minds and spirits just as much as our bodies. Together, we learned to face life's challenges by finding a balance, and making sure we were looking after our whole selves.

For Clayton and me, our belief was a big source of strength. It helped us keep going when things got tough, reminding us that we're not alone in our struggles. This kind of strong faith has been a support for many African American families for generations, helping them get through tough times by keeping their spirits uplifted.

Lately, more African American people are starting to embrace this whole-person approach to health, which is really about waking up to how powerful it is to take care of our mental, physical, and spiritual health together. It's about the whole community supporting each other, sharing our wisdom, and pushing for changes that make sure everyone has equal chances to be healthy. This is a big call to action for all of us to help make the health care system better and more fair, especially for

African American folks, making sure everyone gets the care they need for their whole selves.

Thinking about Clayton's journey and what it means for all of us shows that true health is more than just not being sick. It's about finding a balance that includes our minds, bodies, and spirits. This way of looking at health, which is all about supporting each other and drawing on our community's strength and wisdom, opens the door to healing and being powerful together. By embracing this idea, we keep Clayton's memory alive and move closer to a world where everyone can be their healthiest selves.

Lessons from Clayton's Journey

Clayton's health journey, woven through the fabric of his life's story, offers profound lessons on the intersections of health, wealth, and systemic disparities. His experiences reflect not only personal resilience but also highlight the broader health challenges that disproportionately impact the African American community.

Clayton's encounters with the healthcare system, especially as a veteran exposed to harmful chemicals, underscore the urgent need for healthcare reform that addresses the unique challenges faced by African Americans. His struggle for proper care and recognition of his service-related health issues exemplifies the systemic barriers that many African Americans confront within the healthcare system. These challenges include delayed diagnoses, inadequate treatment, and the long-term impacts of racism and discrimination on health outcomes.

Clayton's story teaches us the importance of advocacy and perseverance in the face of these systemic challenges. It underscores the necessity for African Americans to be informed, proactive participants in their healthcare. Advocacy extends beyond the individual to the community level, highlighting the need for collective action to push for a healthcare system that is equitable, accessible, and responsive to the needs of all its users.

Moreover, Clayton's journey illuminates the value of holistic health approaches that integrate mind, body, and spirit. This perspective is crucial in addressing the multifaceted nature of health disparities affecting African Americans. By embracing holistic health practices, including mental health support and community wellness initiatives, we can better support individuals and communities in achieving optimal health and well-being.

Clayton's legacy is a call to action to prioritize health as a fundamental aspect of wealth. It challenges us to consider how we, as individuals and communities, can work towards a future where health disparities are eradicated. By advocating for systemic change, promoting holistic health practices, and supporting one another in our health journeys, we honor Clayton's memory and contribute to building a healthier, more equitable society.

The lessons from Clayton's journey are clear: health and wealth are inextricably linked, and achieving balance between the two requires addressing the systemic barriers that disproportionately impact African American communities. By learning from Clayton's experiences and advocating for holistic, equitable approaches to health, we can pave the way for a future where all individuals have the opportunity to thrive in health and prosperity.

A Balanced Legacy

In weaving together the threads of Clayton's journey with the broader narrative of health and wealth in the African American community, we've uncovered essential truths about the harmony between physical well-being and prosperity. Clayton's life, marked by resilience in the face of systemic health disparities, leaves us a legacy that is both a challenge and an invitation.

Clayton's legacy invites us to embrace a holistic vision of prosperity, one that recognizes health as the most precious form of wealth. It calls on us to advocate for a healthcare system that is equitable and just, one that acknowledges and addresses the unique challenges faced by African Americans and other marginalized communities.

Advancing health equity requires us to be active participants in our health care, informed advocates for ourselves and our communities, and supporters of policies that promote access to quality care for all. It demands that we break down the barriers that prevent so many from achieving their fullest health potential.

Living Clayton's legacy means prioritizing our health and the health of our communities, recognizing that true success is not measured by material wealth alone but by the richness of our physical, mental, and spiritual well-being. It means building upon the foundations Clayton laid, striving for a balanced life where every individual has the opportunity to thrive.

Balancing Prosperity

As we draw the curtains on this chapter of our journey, "Balancing Prosperity: The Wellness of Success," Clayton and I reflect on the intertwining paths of health and wealth, recognizing their profound impact on our lives and the community we hold dear. Our narrative, enriched by personal experiences and collective wisdom, underscores the essential truth that true prosperity encompasses much more than financial success—it is deeply rooted in our well-being, in the harmony of mind, body, and spirit.

Our journey together has taught us that the essence of true wealth lies in the health and happiness of ourselves and our loved ones. This realization has guided us to prioritize our well-being, understanding that a balanced life is the foundation upon which we build our dreams and aspirations. It is in this balance that we find the strength to pursue our goals, support each other, and make a lasting impact on our community.

Clayton's enduring legacy, coupled with our shared vision, has been a beacon of hope and a source of inspiration for many. It is a legacy that transcends the material, emphasizing the importance of nurturing our physical, emotional, and spiritual health as the cornerstone of true prosperity. Our commitment to this holistic approach to wealth has not only enriched our lives but has also empowered those around us to seek a similar balance in their own journeys.

The role of our community cannot be overstated. It is within this vibrant connection of lives and stories that we have found the support, encouragement, and love necessary to navigate the challenges and celebrate the victories along the way. Our community has been our strength, reminding us that together, we can overcome any obstacle and achieve remarkable feats.

Action Steps for a Balanced Legacy

I offer the following action steps to inspire and guide those who wish to embark on their own journey toward balanced prosperity:

- **Prioritize Well-being:** Make your physical, emotional, and spiritual health a priority, recognizing that true wealth is rooted in well-being.

- **Seek Harmony:** Strive for balance in all aspects of life, understanding that harmony between work, family, and self-care is essential for lasting success.
- **Build Community:** Cultivate a supportive network of family, friends, and community members who share your values and aspirations.
- **Embrace Legacy Building:** Consider the legacy you wish to leave, focusing on the impact you can have on the well-being and prosperity of future generations.
- **Live with Purpose:** Pursue your goals with intention and purpose, knowing that every step taken in health and happiness contributes to a richer, more fulfilling life.

As Clayton and I continued our journey, we did so with the knowledge that our shared story is but one thread in the larger fabric of our community. Our story is a story of love, resilience, and the pursuit of balanced prosperity—a story that we hoped would inspire others to weave their own narratives of health, wealth, and success. Although Clayton is not here with me, we made a promise and I ask that together, you the reader, and me, Lucy, build a legacy that celebrates not just what Clayton and I hoped to achieve but that it is achieved with wellness and prosperity in perfect balance.

11

The Echoes of Empowerment - Voices of the Vanguard: Leading with Purpose"

AFFIRMATION:

"In the woven strands of our community, we find the strength of unity and the warmth of shared stories. Together, we affirm our commitment to nurturing a legacy of love, support, and collective empowerment. We acknowledge that our individual threads, each unique in its color and texture, contribute to the beauty and resilience of the whole. We celebrate the beauty of our lives, rich with the patterns of our experiences, and we pledge to continue weaving this legacy with threads of compassion, understanding, and unwavering support for one another. United in purpose and bound by our shared journey, we move forward with the knowledge that together, we can create a future filled with hope, love, and endless possibilities."

Promises Kept

I kept my promise. I finished the task I was assigned. It was sometimes difficult but I always felt supported by Clayton. I found the strength of shared stories, the resilience of shared struggles, and the joy of shared victories. This has encouraged my soul and is an homage to the collective spirit that defines our journey. I hope that you too will be strengthened by the profound impact of togetherness in sometimes overcoming adversity and building a legacy of empowerment anchored in love.

Our story, deeply entrenched in the ethos of our community, reflects a journey of love, support, and mutual growth. Clayton and I always believed in the power of togetherness, not just as a couple but as a family and as active members of our community. This belief was been our guiding star, helping us navigate the complexities of life, celebrate our achievements, and face our challenges with a united front.

The essence of our journey is not just about the paths we've taken as individuals but about the roads we've paved together, alongside our community. It's about the moments of joy, the periods of struggle, and everything in between. It's about understanding that every challenge we've faced and every victory we've celebrated has been amplified by the support, love, and shared vision of our family and our community. It was not shared by all but nothing in life is 100% except for God.

Our journey, Clayton's and mine, within the colorful layers of our community, serves as a testament to the profound belief that unity and shared experiences are the bedrock of strength and resilience. As Helen Keller once eloquently stated, "Alone we can do so little; together we can do so much." Our story is one of togetherness, a partnership fortified by an unwavering faith in God and each other. This unity was our sanctuary, a haven where we drew strength and courage to face the world's trials. The challenges we encountered, both personal and communal, were met with a shared resolve that only deepened our connection. It was in this togetherness that we discovered the true essence of empowerment - the ability to uplift not only ourselves but those around us.

Life, in its essence, is a mixture of contrasting colors, each shade representing the joys and sorrows, victories and defeats that define our existence. Clayton and I, like any couple, navigated the spectrum of these experiences. Yet, it was in our commitment to facing them together that we found our greatest strength. Our journey was not devoid of challenges, but together, we transformed obstacles into opportunities, and despair into hope.

Our love story, transcending the boundaries of the physical world, continues to evolve. The chapters of our lives, filled with laughter, tears, dreams, and achievements, are bound by an unbreakable bond that defies separation. Though Clayton may no longer walk beside me in the physical realm, our spirits remain intertwined, our legacy unending.

The essence of our bond, rooted in love and mutual support, became a beacon for our community. It demonstrated the transformative power of togetherness, the beauty of shared burdens, and the joy of collective victories. Our lives, intertwined with those we touched, illustrate the profound impact of unity, the significance of each shared moment, and the enduring strength derived from being part of something greater than ourselves.

As we connected the narrative of our lives into the broader community, we contributed to a legacy that transcends individual achievements. It's a legacy built on the foundation of faith, love, and togetherness, reinforced by the stories we share and the lives we touch. In this mosaic of experiences, every thread is vital, every color vibrant, and every pattern meaningful. Together, we created a masterpiece that celebrates the strength of community and the unbreakable bonds of shared humanity.

Celebrating Our Journey

In the heart of our shared journey, Clayton and I found that the essence of our lives together was not merely in navigating the trials we faced but in celebrating each moment of joy, love, and achievement. This celebration was not just a reflection of our happiness but a testament to the resilience, love, and unwavering support we had for each other and our blended families. Our story is a vibrant thread in the broader tapestry of community, exemplifying how unity, love, and our faith in God created a legacy that transcends individual experiences.

Our lives together were a symphony of shared values, with each note resonating with the importance of faith, family, and community. These values were the cornerstone of our relationship, guiding us through life's ebbs and flows with grace and strength. Despite the inevitable challenges that life presents, our commitment to these principles never wavered. Instead, they became the source of our resilience, enabling us to face each obstacle with a shared resolve and emerge stronger, together.

The power of our togetherness was evident in every aspect of our lives. It was in the quiet moments of reflection, in the joyous celebrations of our achievements, and in the solemn periods of grief and loss. Through it all, Clayton always had my back, and I, his. This mutual support was the bedrock of our relationship, a constant reminder that no matter what trials we faced, we would not face them alone. Our togetherness was a beacon of hope, not just for us but for our family and community, illustrating the profound impact of love and dedication.

Life, in its infinite complexity, presented us with trials that tested the very fabric of our bond. Yet, it was through these trials that the depth of our love and the strength of our partnership were truly revealed. When one of us faltered, the other stood strong, a pillar of support and understanding. This dynamic balance was the key to our resilience, allowing us to weather the storms of life with unwavering faith in each other and in the future we were building together.

Our love story, though marked by the physical absence of Clayton, continues to thrive in the spiritual realm. The chapters of our life together may contain moments of sorrow, but they are overwhelmingly filled with love, laughter, and the unwavering belief in the power of our union. Our story, like our wedding rings, is unending, a testament to the eternal nature of true love and partnership. It is a story that continues to inspire, a legacy of togetherness that remains a guiding light for our family and community.

The legacy we built together is woven into the very fabric of our community, a legacy that celebrates the power of shared stories, values, and dreams. It is a legacy that transcends the individual, encompassing the collective journey of our families, friends, and community members.

As I reflect on our journey together, it is clear that our greatest achievements were not in the accolades we received or the challenges we overcame but in the love we shared and the strength of family that surrounded us. What a celebration of togetherness, a testament to the strength found in unity and the enduring power of love. It is a story that continues to inspire, a legacy that will forever be woven into the hearts of our family, friends, and the community that we love.

The notion of a perfect couple is a myth, a fanciful idea that does not hold up against the reality of life's complexities. Yet, Clayton and I found perfection in our imperfections, embracing each other wholly and without reservation. Our love was not diminished by flaws or disagreements; rather, these elements enriched our bond, adding depth and texture to our shared life. We always felt that our coming together was divinely ordered and destined for success.

Our story, though unique in its path, is unending. It continues to unfold, woven into the lives of those we've touched and those who will come after us. Our legacy, while anchored in the love Clayton and I shared, transcends our individual lives. It is a living testament to the belief that in unity, there is strength; in love, there is resilience; and in community, there is hope.

As we look to the future, our legacy serves as a beacon for the next generation, inspiring them to carry forward the values of love, unity, and community engagement. It is a call to action, urging them to add their own stories into the flow of the community, to contribute their threads to the ever-expanding mosaic of shared experiences and collective dreams.

In the heartfelt conclusion, I, Lucy Stewart Desmore, honor the memory of my beloved husband, Clayton, by reflecting on the richness of community and legacy we've nurtured together. Through the lens of our shared experiences, challenges, and triumphs, this narrative is a testament to the enduring power of love, the importance of community, and the transformative impact of leaving a legacy that transcends time.

I find solace in the knowledge that Clayton's legacy lives on, not just in the memories we shared but in the continued vibrancy of the community we loved. Our journey together may have reached its physical end, but the path we carved remains a guiding light for those who walk it after us. Let this chapter serve as a reminder of the power of togetherness, the importance of legacy, and the enduring impact of a life well-lived. Together, we have produced a beautiful quilt of many colors that will continue to inspire, comfort, and unite, a legacy of love and empowerment that will resonate for generations to come.

As Clay would say, *"Keep looking up. That is where you will find the answers".*

Clay - Back in the day

Clay - Back in the day
Lucy Desmore

I Thought About You Today - Jozie B

I thought of you today,
but that is nothing new.
I thought of you yesterday
and days before that too.
I think of you in silence,
I often speak your name.
All I have are memories
and your picture in a frame.
Your memory is a keepsake
from which I'll never part.
God has you in His arms,
I have you in my Heart

You are Missed
Bethune Publishing

Who is Lucy Stewart Desmore

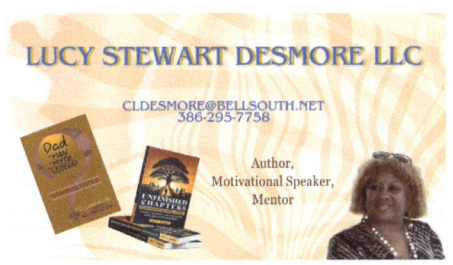

Lucy Stewart Desmore: A Trailblazer in Real Estate and Community Empowerment

Lucy Stewart Desmore is more than just a name; she is a vibrant force in the world of real estate and community service, embodying the spirit of empowerment and resilience. With a life as dynamic as her career, Lucy's story is a testament to the power of determination and the pursuit of excellence.

Born and raised with a zest for achievement, Lucy embarked on her professional journey after earning her MBA from the University of Phoenix. Her intellectual rigor and thirst for knowledge didn't stop there. Lucy leaped into the real estate realm, earning her salesperson license in 2005 and broker license in 2011, showcasing her dedication to professional growth.

Lucy's expertise is as diverse as her qualifications, holding prestigious designations like GRI, AHWD, and ABR. Her recent attainment of the H.O.P.E. Board Certification in 2022 speaks volumes about her commitment to staying ahead in her field.

Based in Volusia and Flagler Counties, Florida, Lucy's work radiates far beyond these borders. As a Broker-Associate, she specializes in various sectors, from luxury properties to commercial real estate. Her role as a Director at the Board of Realtors from 2019 to 2021 reflects her leadership qualities and industry respect.

Lucy's passion for professional development is evident. Completing the Leadership Academy sponsored by the Board of Realtors in 2016 was a milestone, furthering her influence in the industry. Her dedication to community service is unparalleled, earning her the title of Community Service Person of the Year twice, in 2016 and 2022.

As the founding member and chairperson of the Housing Opportunities Committee, Lucy has been instrumental in driving initiatives that make a real difference. Her recognition as one of The News Journal's most influential women in Business in 2018 is a nod to her impactful presence in the community.

Her involvement doesn't end there. Lucy is a fervent supporter and committee member of various events like the Housing Fair and Community Resource Fair. Her advisory role at Allen Community Development, Inc., particularly at Restoration House, highlights her commitment to social upliftment.

Lucy's affiliation with Sigma Gamma Rho Sorority and the Bethune Cookman-Women's Advisory Board further showcases her dedication to empowering women and contributing to her community.

Her personal motto, "You Want Something? Go Get It, Period! Nothing After the Period except Excuses!" mirrors her relentless drive and no-nonsense approach to life and career. Lucy is not just about words; she's about action.

Away from her professional commitments, Lucy is a beacon of vitality. An avid enthusiast of all forms of exercise, she finds joy and rejuvenation in staying active. Her love for music, especially as a songstress, adds another layer to her dynamic personality.

Lucy was married to the late Clayton Desmore for 20 years and was a devoted partner. She continues to be a dedicated mother to Jason, Selena, and Jeri Michelle and stepmother to Corey Desmore which further accentuates her nurturing and inclusive nature.

Lucy Stewart Desmore is more than a successful real estate professional; she is a symbol of empowerment, a mentor, a community leader, and an inspiration. Her journey, marked by perseverance, excellence, and service, serves as a beacon for all aspiring to make a mark in their professional and personal lives. Lucy's story is not just about achieving success; it's about redefining it.

CONTACT INFORMATION:
Email: cldesmore@bellsouth.net

www.ingramcontent.com/pod-product-compliance
Lightning Source LLC
Chambersburg PA
CBHW040846240426

43673CB00012B/361